How To Make Your Company Famous

By Jon Card

ABOUT THE AUTHOR

Jon Card has worked as a journalist for 17 years and has written regularly for titles including The Guardian, Daily Telegraph and The Times. He is the co-founder of media training company Full Story Media which organises the 'How to Make your Company Famous' events series and the Chief Storytellers' Programme, an audacious plan to make entrepreneurs famous.

Through speaker events and workshops, Jon has taught hundreds of business owners and media professionals about storytelling, the work of journalists and how the press works.

CONTENTS

Introduction **PG 7**

Chapter 1: THE STORYTELLER **PG 15**

Chapter 2: THE HERO'S JOURNEY **PG 30**

Chapter 3: STORIES ARE PACKAGES **PG 71**

Chapter 4: PICTURES, PICTURES, PICTURES **PG 85**

Chapter 5: JOURNALIST REQUESTS **PG 94**

Chapter 6: WRITING THE NEWS **PG 104**

Chapter 7: LET'S GET DIGITAL **PG 117**

Chapter 8: UNDERSTANDING JOURNALISTS **PG 126**

Chapter 9: IT'S TIME TO MAKE YOUR COMPANY FAMOUS **PG 135**

INTRODUCTION

Finding things out and then telling everybody is something I've always enjoyed doing. Perhaps this makes me sound like a terrible gossip? Actually, I think people have a right to know most things. Freedom of information and freedom of inquiry are the hallmarks of a progressive society and, well, yes; I am prone to a bit of gossip.

So, back at the turn of the century, I became a journalist. Since then, one of the main things I've learned is how the media and publishing industry works: what it's like to be inside a newsroom, to work on a magazine, newspaper or website and to publish stories for all the world to read.

I want to take you into the newsroom and help you appreciate the role of the journalist. I want you to understand that, if you learn how to help journalists do their job more easily, if you become a great storyteller, you can become very valuable to them. They will, in turn, contact you, feature you more often in their stories and – hey presto – your company will become famous.

Media advice for beer

I estimate that I've met and interviewed roughly a thousand entrepreneurs and business leaders since I began working as a journalist. Initially, our conversations were very one-sided; I asked the questions and they replied. But, as the years went by, I noticed I was increasingly being asked about my work, journalism and how stories were put together. More and more, I was also being asked for media advice by business owners, media professionals and people working in public relations (PRs).

At first, I was quite happy to exchange media advice for beer and, to be honest, I still sometimes do. But there came a point when I realised that I wanted to refine all my theories, test them out and provide entrepreneurs with truly actionable and useful advice.

Over the past few years, I've advised hundreds of people through my own events, conferences, workshops and my own consultancy, and there are many success stories. I've also worked with progressive PR agencies, helping them to reappraise their approaches and to better understand the role of journalists in the digital age. It's not 2005 anymore, or even 2015. Media is changing very rapidly but there are constants that will remain throughout the coming decades – we all need to know what they are.

Glare of publicity

I've met many great entrepreneurs over the years, but many have failed because they've not learned to tell their stories well. They've conceived an idea, found a gap in the market and developed their technology, but the world didn't find them.

The world's various app stores, incubators, office blocks, sheds, garages and back bedrooms contain many potentially wonderful businesses. More than ever, the world needs them, to lead us out of the increasingly dark and worrying times in which we live.

My contribution in this struggle is to help these businesses find the light of day - or rather the brilliant glare of publicity.

I've been a freelancer since 2009 and, in 2017, my wife Corinne and I set up our business, Full Story Media. So I know first-hand the struggles, stresses and pains of running a business.

I know you're quite possibly cash-strapped and almost certainly time-poor. You're probably reading this book between meetings, on a train or after a long day. But this isn't a very long book. My words will be succinct and instructive. Some sentences are very short.

Getting press for Andy
So where did this all begin?

One day I was sat at home working on my laptop and Corinne came in and said:
"Andy wants me to get him some press - what do you suggest?"

Now, Andy was Corinne's boss and she'd worked as a journalist, too - so this wasn't such an unreasonable request.

We sat down and brainstormed everything we knew about the press, media, journalists and entrepreneurs. I began to reverse engineer my work writing for the national press. I considered my best interviews and what made them work. I thought hard about why I had chosen to pursue certain stories.

I began to look through my journalist files and ask questions:

Which stories had been most successful?

What turned an editor's head?

Why had some interviews gone well and others poorly?

What pisses a journalist off? And what makes them happy?

Why do some businesses gain more publicity than others?

What do famous entrepreneurs have in common?

We created an action plan for Andy's business and Corinne executed it. And... lo and behold... our ideas really worked.

Corinne helped Andy gain coverage in the Financial Times, BBC, The Guardian and a whole host of business titles. She was so successful, her clients wanted her to do the same for them. Corinne began to wipe the floor with other PR agencies while I sat in the background, Svengali-like, chuckling away.

It became a buzz to set things in motion and then see our efforts plastered across the big pages of a newspaper or on a TV screen. We began to augment our knowledge with first-hand experience. Corinne was the PR supremo and I was the journalist playing for the other side. We knew we'd hit upon something great.

We were concocting a heady mixture of winning formulas, strategy, media savvy and mysterious, tantalising black magic - ok I'm joking about the last bit, but it was really cool.

But what were we going to do next? We didn't want to run a PR agency, so what? The answer: we did nothing at all, we were stuck. We'd hit upon something really exciting, but we weren't sure about how to turn it into a proper business. So I continued to work as a journalist and Corinne carried on working for Andy who, by now, was using the publicity to attract buyers for his business.

A very cool moment

Many months went by, until I was travelling with a group of entrepreneurs aboard the Clean and Cool Mission. This trade mission, run by Stronger Stories, links clean tech and renewable energy businesses with investors. It also teaches entrepreneurs the power and importance of storytelling; there are many parallels between pitching to investors and speaking to journalists.

During this press trip, I met a long line of incredibly bright and capable entrepreneurs - many had PHDs, professional qualifications and years of business experience. Yet they were asking me many questions about my work as a journalist and how the media functions. I was suddenly feeling very in-demand and realised I had much to offer these ambitious companies - it was quite a boost to my ego.

The founders of Clean and Cool, Guy Pattison and Will Hill, decided to set up a journalist Q&A session with myself, other journalists and the entrepreneurs. It was a great meeting of minds of people from very different backgrounds: entrepreneurs, scientists and the British media.

One of the things that surprised me was how little many of the entrepreneurs really knew about the press. It occurred to me that, if people as smart as this didn't know much about journalists and the media, then many others didn't, either. Also, I was rather taken by just how interested people were in the work of journalists.

I realised then that I wanted to do more to help entrepreneurs to tell better stories about themselves and enable them to gain press, publicity and investment. Corinne and I decided to run our own events and workshops offering media training sessions for entrepreneurs. She quit her job, said a fond goodbye to Andy, and we took the plunge and launched our own business.

Making Entrepreneurs Famous

The first 'How to Make your Company Famous' event was held in October 2017 and I've presented it dozens of times since then. It has reached hundreds of entrepreneurs and media professionals. The feedback we've had has been tremendous and we've had some brilliant companies attend. People described the events as 'insightful', 'inspirational' and 'candid', as well as 'entertaining' and 'fun'.

Crucially, many people have gone on to gain press and publicity for their businesses following the advice we've given. However, it hasn't all been plain sailing. Running events has been a challenge and they are a hellish way to make money - venues, catering, partners - were logistics a pair of journalists had never considered.

But these events them we've found supporters and allies. Entrepreneurs such as Caspar Craven, Carl Reader and Sophie Devonshire have provided us with superb advice. In turn, we've helped each of them gain press and publicity for their businesses in the national and international press. And I've helped a lot of other people, too.

How this book will help make your company FAMOUS

This is a book for entrepreneurs hoping to gain a toolbox of clear, specific and actionable insights into the media that will bring fame and fortune for their companies. If this sounds like you, please keep reading.

How to make your company famous is borne out of experiences I've had working as a business journalist for over fifteen years and counting. During that time, I've met and interviewed countless entrepreneurs who, just like you, knew that getting regular, positive press coverage could transform their companies' prospects.

I've worked inhouse on magazines and websites, commissioned features and headed up news teams. As a freelancer, I've written hundreds of articles for titles including The Guardian, Daily Telegraph and The Times. Journalism has opened up my world. It's given me enormous access to business leaders in the UK, United

States and many other countries. Being a journalist has meant I've been able to ask many questions and seek answers from the brightest people on the planet.

So, this is a book that has been 15 years in the making and the ideas contained have been heavily road tested. It offers a look under the lid of what takes place in media land and provides a lot of advice on how to make the most of it.

But I'll finish on a word of warning:

This book will help you gain publicity; media attention can come very quickly and have a huge impact on your company.

Be ready.

Best of luck with your business.

Jon Card

THE STORYTELLER

I always start my media training sessions with the following questions:

What is a journalist?

What exactly do we do?

How should entrepreneurs and business owners think about us?

There's much debate about the exact role of a journalist. In truth, if you asked ten journalists to describe their job, you'd get ten different answers. And, if you asked ten members of the general public, you'd get ten more - including some less-than-polite replies.

Some consider journalism to be a profession - I don't agree. Some suggest it is a trade - I disagree even more.

But most in the game, whatever their specialism, would broadly agree with this:

Journalists are storytellers.

No matter which section they work in - business, fashion, sport or politics - whether they are print writers or TV broadcasters, they all tell their audiences stories.

Importance of stories

Humans love stories. Stories are used to inform, educate and entertain the masses. They are used to pass knowledge on down the ages and, ultimately, help societies to learn from their mistakes and evolve. From stories around the fire in pre-literate oral cultures, through to the invention of the World Wide Web and social media, humans have always needed stories and, therefore, storytellers. I really don't know what the future of media is. Will newspapers survive? Will there still be journalists in 2050? It's really anyone's guess. What I am certain about is that humans will want and demand stories. Stories have impact. Stories have power. Stories are human.

Before his death, Apple boss Steve Jobs declared:

> *"The most powerful person in the world is the storyteller. The storyteller sets the vision, values and agenda of an entire generation."*

Boom. That's quite a statement from one of the world's most recognisable entrepreneurs. One who, of course, was one heck of a storyteller himself. But he's not the only famous entrepreneur to attest to the awesome power of storytelling. How about this from Virgin founder Sir Richard Branson:

> *"Whatever you're trying to sell, storytelling is the most powerful thing you can do."*

If you've ever read a book by Branson or seen one of Jobs' awesome product launches, you'll have witnessed a masterclass in storytelling. They are highly charismatic business leaders who have achieved great success. But I will argue here that it is not simply their success that has made them famous; there are many very rich entrepreneurs that most people have never heard of. Nor are great storytellers endowed with a special charisma from birth. Storytelling is a talent that can be learned, honed and mastered.

Back to the journalists

Journalists are storytellers and often so are great entrepreneurs – this is no coincidence. Journalists are on the hunt for stories and media savvy entrepreneurs learn how to provide them with what they want. Helping journalists to do their job is a key lesson for all entrepreneurs to take on board.

Journalists play a very important role, as stories have always played a key and central part in human societies. But it also makes them very unpopular with those who want to control the narrative and find the journalists' work to be inconvenient. Technology is also rapidly changing the way journalists operate and is destroying the business model which supports news titles. But, ultimately, our game remains the same – we are here to tell stories.

Entrepreneurs with stories

Because journalists are storytellers, they seek out tales to tell. So, when you meet one, they are probably attempting to gauge what your story is and whether they want to repeat it to their audience.

It is therefore essential for entrepreneurs and business owners to be able to tell stories about themselves. Indeed, one of the things that famous entrepreneurs all have in common is the ability to communicate their personal story.

Media savvy entrepreneurs create stories about themselves which they deliver with ease. These stories have the effect of pre-empting dozens of potential questions and saving both the interviewee and the journalist time. Saving a journalist time is always a smart move as they are busy, usually on deadline and, just like everyone else, enjoy convenience.

Deserving interviewees

Business owners want press and publicity – why wouldn't they? If you've worked hard to create a product, have tapped into customers' needs and genuinely believe that the world should know about what you do, it's understandable that you might like a journalist to write a story about you and for it to be published in a newspaper.

Many business owners I've met over the years feel that they deserve publicity. They passionately and genuinely believe in their companies and sometimes feel a sense of indignation that nobody is writing about them. I regularly receive emails from budding entrepreneurs keen to tell me all about their latest endeavours.

I reply to those I can. But business journalists have busy inboxes. Sadly, there is just not enough time in the day to answer even half the emails I receive.

Media coverage is one of the fastest, cheapest and most effective ways to get your company or organisation noticed by the public. There are many notable examples of companies that have used the media to grow their businesses - I'll be featuring many here and revealing their techniques and strategies.

There also seems to be a close correlation between companies gaining press and those that find investment. Some media savvy businesses achieve tremendous valuations; investors like to back companies that they have already read about in the business sections of their favourite newspapers and online portals.

PR companies

In order to gain publicity, many organisations hire expensive PR and marketing agencies to promote their enterprises. Sadly, some end up disappointed with the results. As a journalist with over 15 years' experience working in the national media, I've met more PR and marketing people than I can remember. The PR and marketing industry is vast, but also incredibly mixed in terms of talent. It is no slur on the industry to say that some agencies are far more capable than others at gaining coverage for their clients.

If you were to spend time sitting in a newsroom listening to journalists, you might very well hear them moaning about the work of PRs or, indeed, the behaviour of their clients. I'll admit to making the occasional contribution to such discussions. The majority of press releases never get beyond a journalist's busy inbox; they are ignored or deleted. Some could have been more successful if they had been edited and amended, but many are non-starters. PRs are often accused by journalists of wasting their time by 'flogging dead horses', 'polishing turds', 'selling coals to Newcastle' and all the rest. To be honest, I feel sorry for a lot of them, they're mostly nice people just trying to make a living. Many PRs actually do know very well what does and doesn't work in media land, but they're put under pressure from their clients or their bosses to create things that are bound to fail.

The PR industry should welcome this book as I am advising entrepreneurs and business leaders on what's really important: telling a story, understanding the role of a journalist and helping them to do their job. This book has not been written to focus on the failings of the PR industry. Nor are we to assume that every bad campaign is down to a poor agency. In fact, many companies fail to gain press coverage because they fail to listen to their media advisors. This book is designed to help companies that want to DIY their own press, avoid expensive agencies or simply to understand how the media works.

A trading business that follows the steps I suggest here ought to be able to gain a substantial amount of publicity, including coverage in the national press. It'll take some time and effort – there are no quick fixes – but if you're an entrepreneur, you'll know that anyway.

Business owners need to recognise the role they have to play in telling their story to the media. Over the years, I've met and heard of leaders of organisations who simply order their teams to 'get some press', without understanding the role they play in developing and championing their own story. The CEO or MD of a company has a vital role in press relations; PR is not something which can be outsourced completely. I don't believe business owners should ever hire a 'head of PR'; that role is already taken, it's your role.

Journalists rely on interviews with key figures and take quotes from authoritative sources – CEOs, managing directors, chairmen, founders, presidents. Take a look in the business sections of any major newspaper or any illustrious economic title – Financial Times, Wall St Journal, Bloomberg – you'll see the majority of interviews are with the heads of organisations. The people I interview are typically entrepreneurs – founders, co-founders, directors. By contrast, I rarely interview the head of marketing or sales, so don't make the mistake of thinking they can 'handle your press' for you.

Chief Storytellers

Entrepreneurs that gain regular press and publicity are their company's Chief Storytellers. The Chief Storyteller realises the power that stories contain. They embrace their own story, realise it is their most potent piece of intellectual property (IP), appreciate the role of journalists, help them to do their job, gain tonnes of publicity and use it to grow their businesses.

As a journalist, I estimate that I've interviewed in the region of a thousand entrepreneurs; on average one or two a week for the past 15 years. The vast majority of them were not 'Chief Storytellers' as described above. Many, I'd struggle to remember at all, even if presented with the words I wrote about them. But, as I think back on my career, some names do stand out and, without question, the interviewees that made the most impact were those with the strongest stories.

Great examples of entrepreneurs who fit my Chief Storyteller definition include:

Sir Richard Branson
Steve Jobs
Elon Musk
James Dyson
Anita Roddick
James Watt of brewery business BrewDog
and Richard Reed, co-founder of Innocent Drinks

The idea of storytelling as a key part of doing business is well established in Silicon Valley and much of the United States. In the UK, it is also increasingly being recognised as a powerful way to communicate. Storytelling is an innately human thing to do, we are hardwired to react and respond to stories. We can all remember stories we were told as children; we remember stories we are told as adults, too.

How journalists work

You may have read numerous books on 'how to do PR' or 'how to meet journalists'. Some contain good information and ideas, but many are bland lists of 'dos' and 'don'ts'. With this book, I aim to provide both a roadmap and greater understanding of how journalists work.

The most important thing to realise is that journalists are storytellers. If you ask a journalist how to get press, they are likely to respond with words to the effect of 'you need a story'.

The journalist's job is to write a story, but this involves much more than just words. The work of journalists has changed and expanded during the digital age. They no longer simply write the news but also publish, distribute and promote it.

As I'll be explaining in detail, stories are packages, including key components such as a headline, hook, quotes and pictures. Businesses that gain regular press coverage are adept at providing journalists with the components they need to assemble these packages. Throughout this book, I'll provide you with tactics and strategies on how you can gain significant levels of press and publicity for your business. Most of the advice I'll be giving will be from my own experience as a journalist and media advisor.

But I'll also be pointing to examples of companies and entrepreneurs – many of whom I've written about and interviewed personally – that have achieved enormous publicity for themselves. Some of these are the big names I've already mentioned, others are great entrepreneurs who, at the time of writing, are still on their journey upwards, such as the adventurer and explorer Caspar Craven, #BeYourOwnBoss founder Carl Reader and UENI CEO Christine Telyan.

The reason entrepreneurs such as these have gained publicity is not simply because they are successful – in many cases, their publicity came before and aided their success. It is because they have all developed strong narratives for their businesses. Journalists are storytellers and the best way to work with them is to tell a captivating tale.

These entrepreneurs are also very recognisable as they've invested time and money into photography and imagery – another key part of any media strategy. And they've displayed a lot of media savvy and social skills, which can be learned and will be taught here.

It's about you, not the product

Some people want to avoid talking too much about themselves. This is understandable but, if you want your company to be famous, you're going to have to get used to some spotlight on you.

Business owners love to talk about the benefits of their products or services. Sometimes I find myself attempting to interview an entrepreneur and they start delivering a sales pitch. Journalists are not customers, they are storytellers, and a sales pitch isn't a story. Journalists want to know about the people behind the business. We want to know who they are, how they got started, why they do this, what inspired them and where they are going. They're the same questions investment pitch trainers often ask:

"Tell me who you are, what you do, why you do it and how you're going to change the world."

Be human

Entrepreneurs often tell stories about their humble beginnings, their challenges, near disasters and their lack of experience or knowledge. You might think a leader of a business would avoid admitting these kinds of stories. Surely, a CEO would rather talk of their successes? But by admitting to having weaknesses and vulnerabilities, the 'big boss' of a company actually makes themselves more relatable, more likeable – more human. It also makes their stories more interesting.

Who on earth wants to read a tale about someone who effortlessly found their way to fame and fortune? However, we find it much easier to relate to a story about someone who started small and then dragged themselves up against the odds. We tend to like such people because we feel we have things in common with them.

Steve Jobs could easily recount how he and Steve Wozniak set up Apple in a garage, soldering parts together to make their first Mac. Anita Roddick would gleefully recount how her first Body Shop was situated between two funeral parlours in a run-down part of Brighton. For entrepreneurs such as this, the big offices, multi-million-dollar sales figures, court cases and all the other 'big business' type activities would come later.

When famous entrepreneurs tell their start-up stories, they are the stories of ordinary people who are taking on the world.

Cut to the chase

I've been interviewing entrepreneurs and business leaders for over 15 years and, if there's one thing I always want to find out as quickly as possible, it's this: 'What does the business actually do?' For many readers, this might seem like the simplest of questions. If you're a hairdresser or a plumber then, no problem, we all know from first-hand experience what your job entails.

But many entrepreneurs - particularly those in the technology space or in new industries - do struggle to explain to outsiders what their work entails. I tend to recommend that business owners find some people outside of their work environment and see if they can understand a 30-second pitch detailing what their company does. It could be your mother or father or a friend from a different industry. Realistically, if they don't understand then a journalist might not, either. But, crucially, the journalist might conclude that their readers won't understand your business and decide not to write about you.

Plain English

The world of work is becoming ever more technologically focused. New categories are being invented every day and business models are often less than straightforward. Silicon Valley is rapidly pumping out new companies with billion-dollar valuations, many of which are pre-revenue. Meanwhile, technology is sounding more like Star Trek every day. When I interview the founders of these companies, my first task is to understand, in layman's terms, what the technology does and then how the company plans to make money from it.

One of the difficulties journalists come up against is that some of the super-bright engineers and technologists we meet are often not used to discussing anything in layman's terms. Indeed, many of us who have spent years working in one industry are prone to forget that those on the outside don't know what we know. When discussing our work, we all too easily start to use jargon, industry acronyms and shorthand descriptions that leave onlookers baffled.

However, it's not just super hi-tech businesses that need to learn how to express themselves simply. Early in my career, I interviewed a banking executive who kept referring to 'KYC'. I let the first couple of mentions pass and when I was certain he wasn't referring to a fast food chain I finally interjected and asked: 'Sorry, what exactly is KYC?'. It stands for 'Know Your Customer' – a key part of banking compliance and terminology. No doubt, in his world, 'KYC' was everyday language, but it's not something the general public would necessarily understand.

In media there are many examples. Marketing people talk of SEO (search engine optimisation) and PPC (pay-per-click), while publishers may be interested in ABC figures (Audit Bureau of Circulations).

Sometimes, jargon is unavoidable or crucial to a story. But when it is used, the journalist will need to define such terms to their readers, and this may affect the flow of a story and detract from its human quality. My advice:

Never dumb down what you have to say, but always express yourself in plain English.

Create a story

Entrepreneurs need to create a short story about themselves that provides a picture of who they are, where they've come from, why they chose to start their business and how they are going to change the world. It's an exercise that will require more than one attempt and probably some input and feedback from others – including your media advisor if you have one. In fact, you'll be honing it throughout your life.

In some ways, a pitch to a journalist is not dissimilar to an elevator pitch to an investor – 'Tell me who you are and how you're going to change the world'. It's a pitch that needs to be in plain English, but not oversimplified. Those listening to it need to be able to relate to you as a human when you tell it. But, like all great stories, it needs to be exciting.

Thankfully, there is a tried and tested format which most media hungry entrepreneurs can use. It's a format that has been used by the likes of Steve Jobs, Richard Branson, Anita Roddick and many other famous entrepreneurs. It's called the 'Hero's Journey', and it's the subject of the next chapter.

CHAPTER 1 EXERCISES

Throughout the book, you'll find challenges and exercises to perform. The purpose of these is for you to be able to outline a useful and straightforward media strategy for your business by the time you've finished reading. If you do the exercises and read this book with reasonable care then you'll definitely get results.

I suggest you take a small notebook and faithfully complete all of these exercises as you go along. If you do so then, I can assure you, you'll be ready to face the media by the end.

#1 Read a 'decent' newspaper every day. I actually recommend a print version because you can read paper faster than on a screen and you're also more likely to read a broader mix of stories. Consider the role of the journalist in each story's creation and ask yourself: *who helped them to write this and how?*

#2 Explain in plain English what your company actually does. Try telling someone unconnected to your industry what you do. Do they understand? Can you tell someone in less than ten seconds?

#3 Make a short list of all the acronyms and jargon used in your business. Define them. Try to discuss your work without using any jargon. Be aware of them the next time you're talking to an outsider.

THE HERO'S JOURNEY

What if I told you there was one simple, successful story format all of the world's best stories followed - a timeless blueprint for how to craft a tale. Furthermore, that you had encountered this format repeatedly throughout your life as it appears in an incalculable number of books, films, plays, magazines, newspapers, fables and tales of old. Yet, weirdly, the majority of people have never heard of it and those that have are unlikely to have truly appreciated its awesome power - including many journalists, PRs and professional storytellers. These would surely be incredible statements. Yet, they are statements which I believe to be true, as do many others. Which leads me to write one more strongly worded statement: all storytellers need to be aware of and to embrace the story arc commonly known as 'The Hero's Journey'.

The Hero's Journey

The Hero's Journey was defined by the American academic and classics scholar Joseph Campbell. In his 1949 work 'The Hero with a Thousand Faces', Campbell declared there was a recurrent theme throughout human history. He described a 'monomyth', which he found occurred repeatedly in stories and legends throughout the ages; a story about an unlikely hero who embarks on a great quest and who, after much pain and suffering, and following a series of trials and encounters, emerges victorious. The 'Hero's Journey' is a uniquely human story which can be found in all manner of places, from the Holy Bible to ancient fables to Victorian Penny Dreadfuls and, more recently, in Hollywood blockbusters.

The Hero's Journey format will be familiar to anyone that has watched the Star Wars films. Indeed, one of Campbell's students at the university where he worked was none other than George Lucas. Lucas used the Hero's Journey format to tell the story of Luke Skywalker, an unlikely hero who eventually overcomes the dark side of the force and overthrows Darth Vader and the evil emperor. Lucas' work and Campbell's theories have inspired many other film makers and storytellers. You'll detect it in many movies created by Steven Spielberg and Disney Pixar, as well as classics such as Alien, The Hunger Games and Rocky. One of the most notable examples of the Hero's Journey in recent times is Game of Thrones - an intricate tale of several heroes and heroines that became a global event.

Campbell didn't exactly invent the Hero's Journey - he discovered or defined it - and others have amended and interpreted the theory since. Key parts of the Hero's Journey are apparent in texts that predate Campbell's work by many centuries, including historical Roman texts and the Bible. Those who know the story of Julius Caesar or King David - who fought Goliath - will be aware of the Hero's Journey. David versus Goliath is a classic Hero's Journey style story, undoubtedly you've heard of it, though perhaps not for many years, yet you still remember it, why?

Heroes

Famous entrepreneurs such as Steve Jobs, Richard Branson and Anita Roddick have all told their personal stories using the Hero's Journey story format. I can't say for sure they were aware of this; the Hero's Journey is deeply embedded in human history and some people seem to instinctively follow its pattern when telling their personal stories. I've been using it for many years, both before and after I learnt of its existence. My first jobs in journalism were won through using a Hero's Journey style pitch, although it wasn't until years later that I realised I'd stumbled upon a winning formula.

Many other successful entrepreneurs and business leaders use this format. Start-up entrepreneurs might very well see parallels between how they began their businesses and key parts of the Hero's Journey.

But before we dip into it, here's one important point: don't worry if you don't feel like a 'hero' - that's fine. Many entrepreneurs don't and are sometimes a bit uncomfortable with the idea. Overall, I've sensed slightly more reluctance from female entrepreneurs than males on this point. We are used to the idea of all-action male hero characters, so it's understandable. However, there is absolutely no reason why female entrepreneurs cannot use the Hero's Journey to create a story about themselves. I've taught many female entrepreneurs how to use it and they've achieved great results. In fact, virtually anybody can tell a story about their life using the Hero's Journey story arc - you don't have to be a business leader.

So here it is, my version of The Hero's Journey, step by step. Follow it and you will be able to create a powerful story for you and your business that the media will love.

The Ordinary World

The Hero's Journey begins in the 'Ordinary World', where we meet our hero. However, our hero doesn't look too inspirational at this point. They are ostensibly unremarkable, an everyman, or perhaps some kind of outsider. Luke Skywalker lives on Tatooine, working on his uncle's moisture farm – he doesn't look like he's about to rule the galaxy. Katniss Everdeen, from the Hunger Games, lives in the lowly 'District 13'. Rocky Balboa is a loser living in the backstreets of Philadelphia.

Early-stage entrepreneurs don't look like they're about to become billionaires, either. Like many Silicon Valley entrepreneurs, Steve Jobs founded his business in a garage, tinkering away with a soldering iron. Richard Branson was running his business from the inside of a phone booth. Anita Roddick set up her first 'Body Shop' between two funeral parlours – she always had a knack for controversy.

Entrepreneurs often see themselves as outsiders and regularly talk about feeling, early on, that they simply didn't fit in. Setting up a business was their means of escape from a world in which they weren't succeeding. The likes of Branson, Jobs and Roddick weren't fit for the corporate world; like many entrepreneurs I've met they concluded that if they were going to be successful they'd have to cut their own path. Branson is dyslexic and his head teacher reportedly wrote that he'd 'either end up in prison or be a millionaire'. Roddick was a perpetual rebel, even after she went into business. And Steve Jobs, well, you probably already know enough about his life story to agree that he was not a corporate person.

Some entrepreneurs like to talk of their humble roots, these are the rags to riches entrepreneurs who pull themselves up by their bootstraps. The working-class heroes who've escaped the confines of their birthplaces to reach greatness. If your background was hard or under-privileged, this is a part of your story which you should embrace. You may have never thought of a tough childhood as a blessing before but, as an entrepreneur, it does add to your story.

Entrepreneurs also make use of their lack of experience – yes, really - their lack of experience. James Watt, who founded the beer and brewery company BrewDog in 2009, loves to remark how he had no experience prior to founding BrewDog and had previously worked as a fisherman. His clever use of storytelling, his positioning of his business as a 'punk brewer', in stark contrast to 'big, corporate brewers', has greatly aided his company's growth into an enterprise worth over $1bn in less than 10 years. BrewDog has been funded by several crowdfunding campaigns - 'equity for punks' - that enabled members of the public to buy into the BrewDog business. But first, they had to buy into the BrewDog story and brand.

Technologists such as Sir James Dyson, who created the eponymous vacuum cleaner, never claimed to be highly gifted. Dyson talks instead about the effort he had to put in to be successful. He almost seems to revel in the rejections, the setbacks and the unlikely nature of his success.

In short, famous entrepreneurs don't tend to boast about their astounding backgrounds. They often do the exact opposite and describe someone who seemed unlikely to succeed. The first stage of the Hero's Journey is to describe where the journey begins, and it starts somewhere quite ordinary. This will help the audience relate to you as we've all lived in the ordinary world. Well, most of us.

The Call to Adventure

So, we've met our hero and we are wondering where this story is going to go. Something happens. The world suddenly changes for them. Maybe there is a chance discovery, a eureka moment, a lightbulb turns on in their minds or they experience some kind of awakening. Perhaps our entrepreneur spots a gap in the market or has a sense that things can be done differently. For Luke Skywalker, it was discovering the Force; for Katniss it was when her sister's name was pulled out of the hat and so she stepped forward to take her place in the arena; for Rocky Balboa it was the surprise opportunity to fight the world champion Apollo Creed. This is the Call to Adventure.

Our entrepreneur is about to begin their journey to change the world. Guy Pattison, CEO of Stronger Stories, always encourages entrepreneurs to think about 'why they are in business'.

"We are all used to telling people 'what we do'. But the really important question is 'why we do what we do'," says Pattison. "The key to a strong story and understanding a business is for the entrepreneur to speak of what motivates them. What was the moment they realised they needed to take this path? How are they trying to change the world?"

Some entrepreneurs are motivated by an overwhelming desire to fix a particular problem. But many entrepreneurs in the technology space chance upon a new idea or make a surprise discovery when they are tinkering in the lab or their workshop. They realise their discovery's potential and embark on a mission to bring its power to the world.

For some entrepreneurs, this can be a single moment, for others it's a collection of happenings. Either way, they begin to see the world differently, and this sets them off on a different course. Journalists love a 'eureka moment'. These help us describe to the reader when, how and why the business came into being. And if you made your invention in your garden shed or your garage then that's a great place to start a story.

There are many examples of entrepreneurial businesses that began life after their founder experienced a flash of inspiration while wandering in the 'ordinary world'.

For entrepreneur Jamie Murray Wells, it was during a trip to the opticians when he was presented with a bill for a new pair of glasses and was taken aback at the price. He decided there must be a cheaper alternative and founded the online spectacles retailer Glasses Direct. Murray Wells didn't have much money (Ordinary World), so used his student loan to finance his business.

Richard Reed, the co-founder and former CEO of Innocent Drinks, once described to me how he was in a juice bar enjoying a smoothie and wondered why it wasn't possible to buy a similar drink from a supermarket. This led him to explore and set -up a business that has had a revolutionary impact on the fruit juice market.

If you don't have a clear call to adventure, don't worry – many business owners don't - but describe as well as you can where your inspiration came from. Something must have got you started and aided in the transition from the ordinary world down the hard path of being an entrepreneur - what was it?

The Refusal of the Call

Archimedes was said to have gone running naked down the road, shouting: 'Eureka'. It's likely to be an apocryphal tale. However, many entrepreneurs pause for a period of reflection, or even denial. After the initial euphoria of discovering something new, the cynical voices of our minds start to gather and doubt sets in. In Star Wars, this is epitomised by Harrison Ford's Han Solo character, who explains that, in all of his experience exploring the galaxy, he's never seen 'The Force'. Many entrepreneurs have to overcome the cynicism of parents, friends, partners and, of course, the market. Entrepreneurs, just like wannabe Jedi knights, experience profound doubt.

So, don't worry if you didn't immediately quit your job to embark on your new venture – this is very common and won't harm your story. I interviewed an entrepreneur called David Toscano, whose restaurant, Cin Cin, had recently won plaudits and awards including a Michelin Bib Gourmand Award. Before he set up Cin Cin, David was a lawyer, which brought great pride to his family. However, for years he yearned to work in the food business and it took him nearly a decade before he quit the corporate world, burned his suits and embarked on his dream. But he did it, as all entrepreneurs do, unlike the majority of people who never pluck up the courage.

When Richard Reed, Jon Wright and Adam Balon set up the smoothie company Innocent Drinks, they were told they'd have to use concentrated fruit juice to make their products. The cynics and doubters told them it was impractical to make smoothies that contained the pulp of fruit. Their products 'wouldn't last', they were 'hard to manufacture' and 'everyone uses concentrate'. However, this was precisely the opposite of their plan, which was to create smoothies from 100% natural ingredients. Investors refused them, as did potential manufacturing partners. But they soldiered on and eventually found partners and investors who helped them to bring their product to market. The trio grew Innocent for many years, inspired many imitators, and eventually successfully exited the business – they proved the cynics wrong.

Doubt, cynicism, scepticism or just useful, critical questioning is something entrepreneurs have to deal with. Journalists may ask a few cynical questions, too – that's our job. Responding to their doubts is part of your role as the leader of your business and it's an important part of your story. Also, remember that cynics are not necessarily against you; many want you to succeed. Indeed, once they are persuaded of your course of action they can become your greatest allies - just like Han Solo.

Allies and Gifts

Stories often revolve around the work of a lone hero and certainly there needs to be a focus for the journalists. Typically, the CEO is the go-to person for interviews, they are the 'Chief Storyteller' of their organisation. But entrepreneurs should never forget their teams when telling their stories. Nobody makes it to the top alone. More than one entrepreneur I've interviewed has quoted the African proverb: 'If you want to go fast, go alone, if you want to go far, go together.'

We all need helping hands along the way. Although in stories, our allies can first appear as cynics, rather than supporters. The classic example is Han Solo in Star Wars telling Luke that, in all his travels across the galaxy, he's never seen 'The Force'. But Luke wins Han over and he becomes his greatest supporter. He's rather like the cynical customer who becomes your greatest exponent.

Acknowledging that you've been helped along the way shows you're human and this will make you more likeable. Remember: all stories are human.

As an entrepreneur, you are constantly in recruitment mode; business owners need to attract customers, staff, investors and anyone else willing to bang their drum for you. It's crucial to reward those who enable your success so that others see it's worthwhile joining your cause.

There are many parallels between pitching to investors and telling stories to journalists. Certainly, investors want to know about your team. It's important for entrepreneurs to be able to offer tales that demonstrate the inner workings and chemistry of their teams. How did you meet? Have you ever been in a difficult situation together and got out of it? When is the team at their best?

Crossing the Threshold

At some point, the Hero's Journey must begin in earnest; they must put the views of the cynics and the feelings of self-doubt to one side and openly commit to their challenge. When I interview entrepreneurs, I want to know when they really set about running their business. For some, the answer might include them quitting their job, taking a loan, investing all their savings into a new technology, selling their house, making a first sale, buying a URL or simply informing the authorities (IRS, HMRC) that they had created a business.

At this point in the story, there's a change of tempo and intensity. For Luke Skywalker, crossing the threshold involved escaping Tatooine in the Millennium Falcon and heading off into outer space. Rocky is now training super hard for the big fight and running up the steps followed by crowds of children. It's when our hero says: 'let's do this', 'bring it on', 'what have we got to lose?'. In the case of Innocent Drinks, the founders crossed the threshold after a successful day selling their smoothies at a music festival. At the event, they asked their customers to place their used drinks cartons into a bin marked 'yes' or 'no' - under a banner asking whether they should quit their jobs and sell smoothies full time. The public voted 'yes' and the trio quit their jobs and founded Innocent Drinks.

For journalists, such an event adds structure to the story. We want to know how you got to where you are today. Crossing the threshold and embarking on your enterprise full time is a key milestone and can be a very interesting story in itself.

Compelling Villains

All great stories have compelling villains and they are a fascinating and infuriating bunch. The Sheriff of Nottingham, The Joker, The Terminator, Agent Smith, The Alien, King Joffrey, Hannibal Lecter and, of course, Darth Vader, who invariably tops every list of great movie villains; We love to hate them and no story is complete without their influence.

The compelling villain is there for our hero to fight against, they are a counterpoint and a clear contrast with our hero's noble cause. They are formidable and seemingly undefeatable, but enemies are very useful to publicity hungry entrepreneurs.

Richard Branson is a master of finding a compelling villain to battle against. When he set up Virgin Atlantic, he pitted it against the nation's flag carrier, British Airways. His radio and media company Virgin Media contrasted itself against the BBC. However, sometimes, in the real world, the Empire crushes the hero; when Branson launched Virgin Cola he ran into an opponent he couldn't overcome in the form of the mighty Coca-Cola.

James Watt, founder of BrewDog, describes his company as a 'punk brewer' and contrasted his company against the bland, commercial beers offered by major brewing companies. A punk is an outsider, a rebel, a misfit and a stark contrast to a corporation. Steve Jobs would quip that he'd 'rather be a pirate than join the navy' - this rebellious spirit runs strong in entrepreneurs.

Entrepreneurs often want to disrupt markets or rage against the status quo. They say things can be done differently, whereas the enemy is the vested interest that likes things as they are. But your enemy doesn't have to be another company. It might be a part of the world you want to change. Your enemy might be pollution, waiting times, punctured tyres or poor childcare.

By considering the enemy, you can think clearly about what it is in the world you want to change; something journalists want to know as well as your customers, clients and employees. Businesses are understanding better than ever before the need to stand for something. People don't want to join businesses simply to make money. Similarly, the general public respond well to brands that offer them a vision of how the world should be. By finding a compelling villain, entrepreneurs can create a 'hero brand'. You won't be the only person in the world who wants to see this terrible foe vanquished. Many 'impartial' journalists will also be hoping you succeed and we have many ways of helping you.

The entrepreneur is the underdog in this battle. It is them against the world. But smart and savvy entrepreneurs learn how to turn this weakness into strength. The great advantage of picking a fight with a much bigger foe is that, if they acknowledge you, they risk giving you credence. But if they ignore you then you become more dangerous. Journalists are only too happy to write about these David versus Goliath type contests; when the challenger wins it is always front-page news.

In sport there are many examples: Muhammad Ali's shock victory over Sonny Liston to win the World Heavyweight title is still recalled nearly sixty years on. The Giants beating the Patriots for the Super Bowl in 2008. Leicester City winning the Premiership title. We enjoy them in business, too. We back the likes of Branson as he steals the big guy's lunch. We love our Silicon Valley heroes who disrupt the status quo. Though, of course, we soon stop loving them when they start to resemble the corporate giants they once opposed. But that's a problem you can deal with later...

Trials and Challenges

The entrepreneur's path is not always easy and there will be many challenges along the way. For a storyteller, this is a good thing. No one wants to hear a tale of effortless success. The ups and downs, the screw-ups, the displays of naivety, these are all part of an interesting story.

To fail is human. Journalists don't like to write glowing

success stories, neither do our readers want to read them. Instead, we'd rather tell a tale of an entrepreneur who's made it big but is also humble enough to recall the times things went wrong.

I've interviewed Michael Birch, founder of social media company Bebo, a few times. Michael has a tremendous success story, having sold his business to AOL for a reported $850m. But his road to success was not an easy one, involving launching several businesses before hitting the jackpot. "I've had more failures than successes," Birch told me when I last interviewed him for The Guardian.

A self-deprecating attitude to success is commonplace among the most successful and famous entrepreneurs. Branson, Jobs, Musk, Gates, Zuckerberg and Roddick have all had periods when the proverbial well and truly hit the fan. It adds to their story, shows they are human and capable of humility - it makes them more likeable.

The Mentor

Wise teachers and mentors also demonstrate the hero's vulnerability and need for guidance. They, too, help the hero through tough times and show them the path to victory. There are many examples of mentors in films: Obi Wan Kenobi, the boxing trainer Mickey in Rocky, Haymitch in The Hunger Games, Doc Brown in Back to the Future.

In real life, entrepreneurs are increasingly recognising the importance of a mentor. They can also be a good topic to write about: 'entrepreneurs reveal the wisdom that led them to success'.

But in the Hero's Journey, the mentor represents another key stage of development for an entrepreneur. As well as having a mentor to help them succeed, the hero who cuts their path through the wilderness subsequently offers others the chance to follow; they become a mentor themselves.

Famous entrepreneurs use their own hero's journey story as a way to act as a mentor to their clients and customers. They were, in effect, their own first customer. They saw a problem and set out to fix it. They've been through the struggles, overcome the compelling villain and reached the end of their quest. But now you, too, who also experience this problem, can join them on their voyage.

Our hero is now in a position to mentor their audience and help them through their own struggles. This story is close to its conclusion.

The Happy Ending

But the story cannot end just yet. This story needs a happy ending. Cynical journalist that I am, I hate to admit this, but it is true: all the best and most popular stories end on a positive note. Audiences want to be left with the feeling that, in the end, good triumphed over evil. They like to see justice being served. We need to reassure our audience that the villain is dead. The good guys have won.

During the final scenes of a film, they want to see gold

medals placed around the necks of their champions, or see their heroes drive off into the sunset. The boy gets the girl and peace reigns supreme once again. Now, the audience can leave the cinema feeling reassured the world is not such a bad place, after all.

For start-up entrepreneurs, the ending of the story may still be far off in the distant future. But where do you see your business in five years' time? What will the world look like if you are successful? If you defeat your compelling villain, how will that change the world? These are key questions you might be asked by a journalist as they put together your narrative.

There are many ways you can end a story. You can finish your tale sadly, horrifically, dramatically, obscurely or even weirdly but, if you want the audience to love it, then it's best to make them smile. Oblique and philosophical endings are common in French cinema but are rarely popular - probably not even in France.

THE HERO'S JOURNEY

There are nine key parts to creating a powerful narrative for your business. The more you include, the stronger the story

1 The Ordinary World
Every story needs to start somewhere and it's best if it begins in a place we can all relate to. This is where we meet our hero - you. But remember, your beginnings are typically humble, naïve or unremarkable. Your journey has just begun.

2 The Call to Adventure

What was the spark of inspiration that got you started? When and where did the lightbulb switch on in your mind? Did you have an Eureka moment? It might have been a lucky accident or a chance meeting. This is when our story begins in earnest. This is WHY you're an entrepreneur.

3 Refusal of the Call

Many entrepreneurs go through periods of self-doubt and indecision. Overcoming the voices of the cynics is a crucial phase.

4 Allies and Gifts

No-one succeeds alone and business owners receive helping hands along the way. This is another opportunity to show some humility. It also shows the gradual development of our hero.

5 Crossing the Threshold

At some point, the entrepreneur must take the plunge and launch their business. This is a big step and can be a great story in its own right.

6 A Compelling Villain

Every great story needs a bad guy. In the business world it might be an established player, the way an industry currently operates, or a problem you are trying to solve. Entrepreneurs are looking to change the world and this means defeating the enemy.

7 Trials and Challenges

Entrepreneurs' journeys are full of struggle. They are part of their development. When everything looks like it is going wrong, drama and tension build in the story.

8 The Mentor
The mentor will help you overcome your doubts, guide you through the challenges and provide you with gifts and tools that you can use to your advantage. The mentor represents the development of the entrepreneur's character and abilities. Later, the successful entrepreneur can take on the role of the mentor.

9 The Happy Ending
The entrepreneur's ambitions are finally realised and our hero wins the day. We all love a happy ending.

Story time

So, as an entrepreneur, you should consider whether your business has anything in common with any of these tales of old. You should then look to craft your own tale, using the Hero's Journey format. As you read entrepreneurial stories, you'll notice parts of the Hero's Journey jump out at you. I've written a number of short profiles and biographies for business owners. They tend to be about 500-600 words long and I include as many of the nine parts as possible. The following stories have all helped entrepreneurs get press and interviews - in some cases they are published verbatim. Crucially, for the journalist, they answer key questions about the entrepreneur - who they are, what they do, *why* they do it and how they are trying to change the world.

HERO'S STORY: CARL READER

The school drop-out turned entrepreneur, business advisor and small business champion

As a teenager, Carl Reader's life didn't look promising, but he has since become a mentor and advisor to some of the UK's largest organisations and companies, as well as chairman of his own company.

Carl Reader dropped out of education at 15 and initially worked as a hairdresser. He later returned to school, gained a clutch of GCSEs and landed a job as a trainee accountant. But adding up rows of numbers wasn't for him.

"I never wanted to be an accountant, but I really enjoyed going out and meeting business owners. That planted a seed in my mind. I wanted to do something over and above adding up numbers and be involved in helping businesses to grow," he says.

Reader joined business advisory firm D&T in May 2002 and proved himself an effective salesman and advisor, bringing in new clients as well as advising them on how to grow. "I was good at sales, liked meeting customers and often trained them on how use new software."

Using loans from his parents and colleagues and "sweat equity", Reader was able to take part in a management buy-out in 2007. He spearheaded D&T's transformation from a small firm with seven staff into a disruptive, innovative business with data and software at its heart. D&T now has over 2500 clients including

Dyno, Esquires Coffee, Molly Maid, Barking Mad, Little Kickers, Anytime Fitness and Card Connection.

In January 2008, D&T became Xero's first European partner and the first outside of New Zealand to help the emerging tech giant shape its offering for the UK.

Reader believes the finance and professional services sectors are going to be heavily disrupted. He says D&T's future lies, not as an accountancy firm, but as an entrepreneurial advisory business.

"I have tattoos and don't wear suits and you'd never guess I was an accountant. But the truth is, soon, nobody will look like an accountant, as it will mostly be software."

D&T was also one of the first accountancy businesses to specialise in a sector – martial arts. "We had a few clients that were martial arts schools and started to build a niche. Being young and male helped, but it was mostly about speaking their language and not going in as an accountant – I was more like one of their mates. I later became a non-executive director of the British Taekwondo Council and helped them raise funding for the Olympics. I can't even do martial arts."

D&T has had a major impact on the franchising sector. Reader realised that the data across a franchise network was immensely powerful as it enabled them to compare key business metrics such as costs, footfall and revenues.

"We began to know the franchisees better than the franchisor did – we saw it all. So the model moved from tax compliance and accounts to where it is now, which is being a data house and advisor. Financials are filled with powerful data. What I love to do is to unlock the magic behind those numbers."

WHY IS THIS A GOOD STORY?

Carl's story contains several key parts of the Hero's Journey. The Ordinary World is well established as he is initially portrayed as a somewhat wayward 15-year-old with few prospects. Although his 'Call to Adventure' is not crystal clear, he begins to realise his business potential and grasps that he can make a success of himself. He family, friends and colleagues are his Allies, lending him cash (Gifts) and holding the door open so he can buy into the business. But he has to work hard, struggle (Trials and Challenges) and he's always something of an outsider, shunning suits and proudly sporting tattoos. His compelling villain is the old-fashioned approach to business and accounting - Carl has arrived to shake things up, take advantage of the data age and offer a new kind of business model. He's been successful and is now leading the way for others - the journey from hero to mentor is complete.

HERO'S STORY: CARLENE JACKSON

"Dyslexia is a gift that's helped me in business"

Carlene Jackson saw the potential of cloud technology early and went on to build a thriving consultancy business with 20 staff. She talks about partnering with Microsoft, staff and apprenticeships and how a 'learning difficulty' has made her a better entrepreneur

"I consider my dyslexia to be a gift that's helped me in business," says Carlene Jackson, founder and CEO of Cloud9 Insight. "If you're dyslexic, you can never truly fail, because you simply accept that succeeding first time may not happen so you're going to have to find a way around the problem."

Indeed, many famous and tremendously successful entrepreneurs are or have been dyslexic; Richard Branson, Lord Alan Sugar, Anita Roddick, Walt Disney and Henry Ford were all reportedly diagnosed with the condition. Research suggests dyslexia is disproportionately found among entrepreneurs. "You learn differently, see the world differently and these things are very useful when you're an entrepreneur," Jackson adds.

Born in Dublin, Jackson moved to Brighton as a teenager and started out in business aged 17, running a catering franchise in a pub. "I learned the hard way that catering is a tough way to make money," she says.

Jackson trained as an air traffic controller, but it was at this time she found out she was dyslexic. "Air traffic control isn't a very good job for a dyslexic like me. If you don't instruct planes to turn the right direction, they might crash, so I abandoned that idea," she laughs.

So Jackson entered the corporate world, learned sales at IBM and moved into the growing field of customer relationship management (CRM) software. "My biggest strength is sales strategy. I'm pretty quick to understand customers, connect with them drive change and help companies set a vision."
But it was when cloud computing began to emerge

that Jackson saw the chance to realise her ambitions and become an entrepreneur. "My brother is a serial entrepreneur, he encouraged me to stop making millions for others and make it for myself. Microsoft, at that time, was getting lots of attention with a cloud-based CRM solution for the UK market, which had previously only been on-premise. I saw there was a big opportunity there, so I seized the moment to start a new business focused on Microsoft Dynamics and have never looked back since."

Carlene founded Cloud9 Insight in 2010 along with Nigel Ridpath, who she later bought out, and has grown to over 20 staff. The company is on target to reach £2m turnover in 2019 and has gained over 600 clients. However, there have been a number of challenges along the way. In particular, transitioning from working with enterprise clients to its SME base.

"We sell to small and medium sized businesses, so it's the owner's money you are spending. I had to quickly learn how to adjust to this as I had only ever sold to Enterprise clients before."

Jackson says the company's close relationship with Microsoft and ability to deliver its solutions has been key. "If you were to call up Microsoft about CRM systems, there's a very good chance they would refer you to us," she says.

The development of staff has always been a big driver for Jackson, with her skills winning her several industry awards for investing in people. Cloud9 is also an apprenticeship provider to the tech industry, having received government accreditation in Autumn 2019.

"I'm proud of the fact that many of the people I have recruited have not worked in the tech sector before and I have coached them to the success they have achieved. I am passionate to help people fulfil their potential and dreams - being an apprenticeship provider will help us achieve this even further."

WHY IS THIS A GOOD STORY?

Carlene's dyslexia is a critical part of her story, as it has been for many other entrepreneurs. It means she's the permanent outsider, who sees the world in a different way. She's also a woman in the tech world - which makes her stand out. She's been through various struggles and setbacks but eventually found her way. Finally, she sees a chance to go it alone and take advantage of the burgeoning cloud software industry. She's been successful and now, through her apprenticeship programme, is mentoring other young people into the tech world. It's a perfect combination of vulnerability and success - she's someone who you enjoy seeing win.

HERO'S STORY: CHRISTINE TELYAN

How toothache led to a web revolution

Entrepreneur Christine Telyan vowed to make all businesses visible online after struggling to find a local dentist. She now runs UENI, a "digital agency for the masses"

Business ideas are often a reaction to a personal problem. For Christine Telyan and Anh Pham Vu, their inspiration occurred while they were searching for a dentist online to cure Anh's toothache.

"I thought it would be easy but actually it took quite a while and a number of calls to find and book an appointment," recalls Telyan, now co-founder and CEO of Ueni.

The bad experience stayed in the minds of the couple and led them to realise that if dentists were hard to find, so were many other types of businesses. "This was the founding moment and we began to look into it in more detail. We realised there were so many local micro businesses that weren't being represented in online search results."

UENI provides a free website and Google My Business listing to all small businesses that want one. UENI's 'freemium' model now sees hundreds of businesses sign up per day.

The business also provides paid services such as a custom domain name, professional email address and listings on trusted, high traffic maps, directories, and social media sites.

The London-based company currently operates in the UK, France, Spain, the United States and India. Telyan says her work is helping small businesses climb up the Google rankings and means small businesses can compete with big brands.

"Our mission is to make all businesses visible online," she says. "Whenever we need to buy things, the first thing we do is search the internet. But by and large, search results turn up chains and franchises, and many small businesses are invisible online."

The couple co-founded the business in December 2014 and in February 2015, Christine quit her job as an oil trader to focus on UENI full time. Later that year, her company gained its first investment of £1.5m from business angels. As of 2019 the company has raised a total of £15m in funding.

But developing a product and business model in such a broad and fragmented market has been challenging.

"When we started, there was a lot we didn't know. We had to find people with tech and coding skills to help us. We went to meet-ups and university fairs looking for talent. Our early hires could have gone elsewhere but wanted to work with us because they believed in our mission. They were also really helpful recruiting others to our cause.

"Another big challenge was finding the right market approach. We started out as a consumer search platform where people could find the cheapest, nearest or best rated service. We then moved over to be a business solution to get small businesses visible online. In the process, we also shifted from direct sales to strictly digital and our current, freemium model."

At the time of writing UENI is signing up over 3000 businesses every day and the rate of growth is accelerating.

"We are an agency for the masses. There is a tremendous unmet need, both here in the UK and globally. Our mission is to make all businesses visible online," says Telyan.

"We want to level the playing for small businesses. For consumers, this means far greater choice when buying locally. For our customers, it means more trade and business growth. And for big businesses that have been taking their customers for granted, watch out."

WHY IS THIS A GOOD STORY?

Christine's story starts in the ordinary world - she's looking for a dentist for her husband. But this leads her into a mission to change the world, helping small businesses overcome the strength of their bigger rivals - classic David vs Goliath stuff. In particular, a lack of visibility online is her compelling villain. But it's a battle still being fought and there were many challenges along the way - finding funding, finding staff and getting the business model right. But Christine is determined to create a better world with a fairer and more balanced internet - good news for both consumers and small businesses.

HERO'S STORY: CASPAR CRAVEN

Caspar Craven: "Divorce among CEOs has become normal - this has got to change."

By his early 30s, Caspar Craven had it all. A university educated technology entrepreneur; this high achiever had even sailed around the world. The only problem: he was bitterly unhappy. His marriage was on the rocks, his work were colleagues at the point of mutiny.

"Every day followed the same, miserable pattern. I was into the office early and stayed late. There was always something that came up that stopped me going home; a proposal to get out, a project to finish, a staff issue to deal with," says Craven.

"My wife was clearly feeling neglected. We were arguing about money, our sex-life was non-existent. We had to focus on our relationship and our two young toddlers, or we would go our separate ways."

Meanwhile, relations with his business partner at tech firm Trovus were also strained. "The crunch came when he pulled me to one side and said: 'either you've got to change or everyone is going to leave – including me'.

"At first, I was angry, and just wanted to fire the lot of them. I was totally driven and focused on my own ambitions. But, after I calmed down, I realised I must be driving everyone mad. I was on course to lose everything."

Meanwhile, things at home were about to take an interesting twist. "Nichola and I came home from a party where a friend had been talking about sailing around the world. We got home and Nichola just said: 'you want to sail around the world, don't you?' Of course, I did, but I didn't want to leave everyone behind. We talked and talked until we came up with a solution: we agreed that we should sail around the world together, as a family."

However, at this point, the Craven family, which also consisted of Columbus age 2 and Bluebell age 4, seemed wholly unsuited for this mission.

"Everyone said we were mad. We didn't have a boat or enough money to buy one, let alone the funds to live at sea for two years. So, raising that money and fixing those problems became our goal. We were going to grow the business, sell it and use the proceeds to fund our adventure."

But the business needed major changes, too.

"The problems I had at work mirrored those at home. We lacked common goals, values and language. I wasn't listening enough. I needed to stop thinking about my own goals and start realising that people at work had their own motivations. I began to learn the importance of team building, at work and also in my family."

Craven began to research successful companies and entrepreneurs. He became intrigued by the work of thinkers such as David Schwartz, Dan Kennedy and Tony Robbins. He recognised the importance of goal setting and also of helping others.

Over the following months, transformation took place at Caspar's home, and at work. The Craven family and the Trovus company created shared values, while also setting individual goals. "We all started talking more, getting on better. Work hours got shorter but productivity and profitability soared."

On 20th August 2014, the Craven family set sail from Southampton for an epic, two-year journey around the globe. How they not only survived, but prospered, is recorded in Caspar's book: 'Where the Magic Happens'. Highlights include power failure mid-way across the

Pacific Ocean and Caspar selling his business Trovus for a seven-figure sum from onboard his ship Aretha.

He now works with business leaders and professionals, ensuring they don't fall into the same traps that nearly ruined his marriage and family life.

"The divorce rate among CEOs is above average – it's become normal. We've accepted the idea that you work hard for years and neglect your family so you can enjoy the benefits later.

"Business leaders are sacrificing their family life for success at work – this has got to change. I teach people to understand they need two teams: one for work and one for family.

"Business leaders need to recognise the importance of others in their lives, to recognise that their own motivations are not the same as those around them. Ultimately, we need to stop working our whole lives for a few days in the sun. It is possible to create a successful business and family life, too."

WHY IS THIS A GOOD STORY?

Although Caspar's story starts off with a strong air of success, we quickly learn he's just as fallible as the rest of us. He's struggling, not happy and failure at home and work is perilously close. He realises this and sets out on a grand mission – one in which he has no realistic prospect of success and most people think is utterly mad. There are many struggles, learning moments but eventually our hero overcomes the odds and emerges with lessons for us all.

HERO'S STORY: DAVID TOSCANO

Cin Cin: The Story So Far... From a street van to a Michelin Award

David Toscano grew up in Sydney in a family of Italian immigrants and came to London in 2005, initially working as a lawyer. He loved the capital's pop-up restaurant and street food scenes but felt there was a lack of choice.

"We looked at the street food scene and thought it was all so macho; burgers, pulled pork and spicy food. We thought there was a gap in the market for something more refined. I wanted to be able to buy the sort of Italian food I loved and ate as a child."

David was not a trained chef and had no experience running a food or restaurant business, but friends and family encouraged him to offer private dining services.

In 2013, he set up Cin Cin in a 1972 Fiat 850 camper van at the Street Diner food event on the Queen's Road, Brighton. "We did £500 of business and met some of our strongest supporters there."

He continued to work part-time as a caterer while also working as a lawyer. However, in August 2014, David met head chef Jamie Halsall and began to work together at events, parties and festivals. At the end of the year he quit his job and committed to Cin Cin.

"Soon after meeting Jamie, I quit my job, burned my suits and committed to it full time. I wanted to create the type of restaurant I wanted to eat in."

Cin Cin's highly acclaimed restaurant opened on Vine St, Brighton in September 2016 and has won plaudits, awards and in September 2018 won the Michelin Bib Gourmand.

"Just a few years ago Jamie and I were standing in a tiny kitchen experimenting with pasta and comparing recipes for Tiramisu. Now we have won one of the most prestigious food awards in the world. It's been an incredible journey.

"Cin Cin serves the simple, seasonal and delicious food. It is the food of my grandparents who hail from Calabria, Italy."

Cin Cin on Vine St is a small but atmospheric restaurant tucked a way in the back streets of Brighton near the Lanes. It has a simple menu: three small plates (antipasti), three handmade pastas (fish, meat, veg) and three desserts. It serves a maximum of 75 covers per day - lunch and dinner.

In January 2018 Cin Cin opened a second premises on the Western Rd in Brighton. Enabling David and Jamie could to expand their menu and serve more customers.

"Our Vine St restaurant is nearly always full so we opened a larger Cin Cin on the Western Rd where we can serve more customers and provide a wider menu. The new restaurant is doing well and we aim to expand the business across the South of England and beyond."

WHY IS THIS A GOOD STORY?

David realised his passion was for food but had to overcome his own personal doubts and the views of his family and find the money to launch his restaurant. He enters a lengthy period of indecision (Refusal of the Call) and, slowly, his allies help him inch his way toward launch. Finally, he crosses the threshold and you can picture his delight as he 'burns his suits'. The grip of normal life, the expectations of others and the corporate rat race have been broken - his enemies defeated. Pasta has never tasted so good.

HERO'S STORY: SIMON PAINE AND ALAN DONEGAN

PopUp Business School: How a rant letter caused an entrepreneurial revolution

Simon Paine was sent to deal with a complaint about Business Link's poor advice. He ended up quitting the government advisory service and founding the PopUp Business School with Alan Donegan.

"I was handed a three-page handwritten letter of complaint and thought - who on earth writes letters by hand?" recalls Simon Paine, now co-founder and CEO of PopUp Business School.

The author of the "rant letter" was Alan Donegan, a serial entrepreneur who felt the advice he'd received by the then government's advisory company, Business Link, was poor.

"It was so bad it nearly put me off starting a business. They told me to write a business plan, do financial projections and take a loan. I remember sitting at home feeling lost and dejected. I didn't want to get into debt, I wanted to start making money," says Donegan.

Paine, who, in 2011, working as Business Link's programme manager, met Donegan at a café to discuss his issues. Three hours later, he emerged thinking that actually Donegan was completely right and that entrepreneurs both needed and deserved a much better service.

"We realised Alan wasn't the only one turned off by the 'traditional' way of starting a business," says Paine. "So we kept on talking and thinking about how to make things better."

In 2011, the pair decided to set up The PopUp Business School to provide a clear alternative to traditional business advisors. The PopUp method focuses on making sales, rather than business plans and debt. It has proved successful, being popular with groups such as the long-term unemployed, people on a low income, students and those for whom English is a second language.

The company's recent impact report found that a quarter of those attending the two-week course launch a business while at the school, with most of those also making their first sale within five days.

But the idea took some hard work and fine tuning before it took off. "Our first event was in a backroom at a timber workshop. Many of those attending didn't really want to be there, they'd been sent by the Job Centre - but we won them over," says Paine.

The PopUp Business School has faced some fierce criticism from those who favour the traditional approach.

"We've been regularly attacked by traditional business advisors because we are the complete opposite of the traditional approach taught by places like Business Link, schools and banks," adds Donegan. "But I'm sick of people who never started a business telling others how to do it. Accountants, teachers and lecturers, who've never run a business, are putting people off with bad advice."

Since 2012, over four thousand people have attended PopUp Business School events and the company has popped up in six countries worldwide. In 2018 it helped launch 680 businesses.

"We've had cake makers, fitness trainers, the long-term unemployed and people who can barely speak English come to our events. You don't need money to start a business, most people just need an idea and someone to show them how," says Paine.

Donegan adds: "We are democratising entrepreneurship to make it possible for anyone, regardless of their starting point, to make money doing something they love. Our mission is to change the way starting a business is taught by removing the need for business plans, and start-up loans and, instead, making the very best, practical business training free to anyone that wants it."

WHY IS THIS A GOOD STORY?

I wrote this story as both Alan and Simon were keen to be involved in the press and media and so it is composed of two overlapping Hero's Journey stories. Simon's Call to Adventure is when he's handed Alan's angry rant letter - a clear indication Alan has already identified his compelling villain - traditional business advice. Together, they go on a journey revolutionising business advice and helping struggling entrepreneurs.

But they start off in a humble way, in the back room of a timber workshop which is, of course, in stark contrast to the government backed Business Link or the plush offices of a traditional accountants. These heroes become mentors to a new generation of entrepreneurs, 'democratising' advice by giving it away for free and helping people from all walks of life achieve their dreams, regardless of how much money they have.

HERO'S STORY: PAULINE DAWES

Pauline Dawes, founder of Somi Trailers, forsaw a transport revolution while stuck on a motorway next to a lorry

Pauline Dawes was sitting in a traffic jam on the M6 with a large truck stopped to her side. She looked under its trailer at the large gap between the wheels and wondered: 'Why aren't we using that space?'

This gave her the inspiration to start up Somi Trailers. The Lincolnshire-based company has developed an innovative new trailer, which has space for an extra six to eight pallets, compared to a standard model. "In a trailer, you are fighting for millimetres – everything is about getting as much cargo in there as possible. I want to make this the new, global standard for trailers," she says. Somi's trailer has an additional compartment underneath. Loads are placed and retrieved from this gap by patented pneumatic systems. Although the truck carries heavy loads, the fuel cost is offset by improved aerodynamics, created as a result of the space beneath the trailer being filled. The business is now working with retailer clients, as well as seeking investment. For Dawes, it's been a long, hard journey.

"It's taken 22 patents, £3m, 10 years of my life and one second mortgage," she says. "But we believe that, if this technology is rolled out globally, we can take up to one in four trucks off the road."

WHY IS THIS A GOOD STORY?

Pauline's Call to Adventure comes while she's sitting in a traffic jam on the motorway – what could be more commonplace than that? She then goes through an arduous struggle to bring her business to fruition – creating patents, raising funds, even mortgaging her house. She puts everything on the line. She's a woman in a male dominated industry, fighting for change. Ultimately, her dream is to take a quarter of the world's trucks off the road – in age of climate change and traffic congestion, that's a meaningful quest. Her challenge continues...

BLUEPRINT FOR SUCCESS

The Hero's Journey is a blueprint for storytelling success. It is an archetypal human story and can be used by anyone to tell a tale. I decided to dedicate just one chapter to it but I really could write far more. Many books have already been written on it with the most important being Joseph Campbell's 'The Hero With a Thousand Faces', originally published in 1949. My take on it is a much-simplified version, for busy entrepreneurs keen to get their stories out there.

The Hero's Journey has tremendous depth and application. It can be used as a whole or broken into parts. The Call to Adventure can be used as an elevator pitch for entrepreneurs. The Compelling Villain is a way to differentiate oneself from the competition. The Refusal of the Call is key to handling objections and convincing others. The Crossing of the Threshold is an important point on your company timeline.

TELL ME ABOUT YOUR BUSINESS

As a journalist, I'm always keen to find out a few key things about my interviewee. I often ask them the question: 'tell me about your business'. If the entrepreneur responds with a simple story, explaining why they decided to start up their company, then I know this is going to be a good interview. The Call to Adventure is a great way to tell an introductory story about yourself or your business. The listener can relate to you straight away as it begins in the ordinary world. Then, there is a transformation and, now, I can understand why you're in business.

Journalists need to know some basic things from every interviewee: who you are, what you do, why you do it and how you're going to change the world.

By reflecting on their own Hero's Journey, all entrepreneurs can answer those questions.

HUMAN STORIES

There are many lessons to be learned within the Hero's Journey. Overall, its main lesson is that stories are about people. Journalists don't want to write about products or services, but they do want to feature those who create them. These people are much more appealing when they seem to be like us: when they display vulnerability, flaws and sometimes fail completely. But, ultimately, we want them to succeed and to be able to help us with our struggles and problems. The hero vanquishes the villain, saves the day and is now our mentor.

CHAPTER 2 EXERCISES

#1 Consider the Hero's Journey. Work through each of the nine parts. Try to define your call to adventure, compelling villain, allies and onwards, moving through every stage of the journey. Don't worry if some parts are less clear than others. Return to this exercise regularly.

#2 Look for examples of the Hero's Journey in films, TV, books and, of course, in newspapers. Start noting your own examples.

#3 Attempt to write your own Hero's Journey story, similar to those above - about 500 to 700 words. If you're not a great writer, get some help, but try to use your own words as much as possible.

#4 Think about how you are helping your clients or customers. Have you become the mentor? Try another version of the Hero's Journey where your customer is the hero and you are the mentor.

CHAPTER 3

STORIES ARE PACKAGES

The journalist's job is to write or create a story. Indeed, journalists are storytellers, but what exactly is a story? When I train business owners and media professionals, what I say to them is this:

> *"Stories are packages. A combination of components such as a headline, standfirst, news angle, facts and figures, body copy, quotes and, the thing so many people forget until the end, pictures."*

Anyone who has ever published a blog or used a content management system should be able to get insight into the modern journalist's job. Writing the main copy is the easy part. Journalists are writers so knocking out the words is something they can do quite easily. It's finding and arranging all the other key components of the story that is the challenging part.

Entrepreneurs that gain regular press coverage are adept at providing journalists with the components they need to create their stories. They appreciate they have a role to play in helping the journalist 'put it all together' and recognise the journalist cannot do it all by themselves. Journalists get the final edit, they compose the words and decide upon the angle of the story. But their options are limited and somewhat decided by what the interviewee gives them to work with.

An easy way to make sense of this process is to break up the different parts or components of a story and appreciate which parts the journalist relies on you for. Then, when you're creating your press materials, you can analyse them separately and ask: 'is this helping the journalist to do their job?'

Key components

A feature or news story contains a number of key components: headline, standfirst, body copy, quotes, facts and figures and pictures. In the digital age, there are also links to other pages and, increasingly, videos are being added to online stories.

It is very important to realise that, if a journalist cannot create or obtain one of these components, it is very likely that the story won't be published. If the journalist cannot conceive of a headline, they can't publish. If there are no usable quotes because the entrepreneur is spouting salesy rubbish or marketing speak then they can't publish. If there are no good quality pictures then the story won't be published, or will be very small, or they will assess whether something from the stock image library will suffice – often, they won't.

All entrepreneurs must realise that stories aren't published because they are worthy. The stories at the front of the newspaper or on the homepage aren't necessarily the most important. There is little justice in what gets published and what doesn't. The decision-making process revolves around firstly, whether the story is of interest to their readers and then, whether it can be practically done. Many good stories never see the light of day because there is a lack of a spokesperson to provide the quotes, a lack of pictures to help the reader visualise the story or a lack of hard facts to justify key claims. In some cases, my interviewees tell me lots of interesting things, but I still cannot conceive of a headline.

So, if a journalist is unable to obtain or create one or more of the components below, then there is a good chance the story won't get published. If you understand these then you're much more likely to get press for your business.

Headlines and standfirsts

A headline is a short sentence which encapsulates the story beneath it. They are always composed of a small number of simple, recognisable and, preferably, 'famous' words. A headline that includes famous words such as 'New York', 'London', Madonna, 'The Queen' is likely attract attention. The verbs of headlines tend to be stout, simple words. I think they are often quite Old Testament biblical; 'Vows', 'Condemns', 'Fights', 'Promises', 'Saves'. I once received a press release entitled 'Update for Platform Xelpha now facilitates Python'. Well, God doesn't facilitate anything - he's much more powerful than that. I've never heard of Xelpha and if there's a python in my story, I want a great big snake, not a computer language. Keep headlines simple.

Often, when a journalist is assessing whether or not to write a story, they are attempting to envisage a headline. Headline writing comes more naturally to some than others. But there is plenty of advice from senior journalists on how to write one.

Emma Sheppard, freelance journalist at the Guardian, has this to say about headlines: "A past editor used to say to me - 'Imagine you've just run to the top of a hill to see a friend you haven't seen for a long time. You only have enough breath to get one sentence out about this story. What do you say?' That's the crux of your story and you should lead your press release with that. I'd put it in the subject line, too."

As Emma suggests, it's very easy to overthink headlines. The best approach is simply to come out with them and then edit according to the rules I laid out above. Thankfully, the final edit of a headline is left to the editor and entrepreneurs don't need to become master headline writers to succeed. But business owners have to understand that a journalist will need to write their story beneath an eye-catching sentence which neatly sums up the story. Without one, there is no story.

Standfirst

Not all stories have standfirsts, but you'll often see them in larger pieces. Standfirsts are the couple of sentences directly beneath the headline that give the reader some further clues as to what the story is all about. The words of a standfirst must be different to the headline. These are the words which didn't fit into the headline, so they dropped down to the line below. For instance, there's been a football match and one side has won convincingly for the first time. The striker had a great day and everyone sees this as a vindication of the manager's strategy. There are multiple ways you can write this headline.

ENGLAND BEATS SPAIN 4-2
KANE STRIKES TWICE IN HISTORIC WIN OVER SPAIN
SOUTHGATE JUBILANT AS CAPTAIN KANE LEADS ROUT
IN MADRID

But if we take the first headline - ENGLAND BEATS SPAIN 4-2 - all of the other words fall into the standfirst:

'Harry Kane strikes twice in historic Madrid victory, as Southgate's new system shows its worth'.

Once again, it is the journalist's job to write this, but if you've put together a press release or blog post then I recommend you follow these rules.

Here's an example of a headline and standfirst from the tech start-up world:

Government backs childcare start-up to create AI platform
MyTamarin is set to become the 'match.com for childcare', having won £100,000 from Innovate UK

So the headline is composed of simple words as well as 'Government' - a 'famous' word. I didn't use the company name in the headline as it is a new and unknown business. Instead, we used the phrase 'start-up' which juxtaposes with Government and AI as artificial intelligence is a hot topic. Quite conceivably, we could have put the £100,000 figure in the headline, but we didn't, so it dropped into the standfirst.

Quotes

Quotes are one of the components a journalist relies on an interviewee for. We can't make them up – well, we shouldn't - so it's vital for the entrepreneur to become adept at providing this key part of a story.

Quotes are really important and can make or break a story. They bring a story alive, give it excitement. Quotes are the voices of people, they have personality, are unpredictable and contain emotion. Stories are about people and the quotes are directly from the people - they are human.

The best quotes sound natural, they aren't polished. The Hero's Journey offers a way to unlock your voice. Entrepreneurs should talk of their struggles and challenges. They should display their humility and admit to mistakes and the fact they are on a journey of self-discovery and improvement. Sadly, very few press releases or statements display any of this. Press releases from the corporate world contain quotes that no normal person would ever say. When businesses make announcements, they have a habit of slipping into marketing speak. Instead of expressing their genuine excitement, for some reason they decide to communicate in the blandest way possible. Marketing speak is anathema to journalists, who always prefer direct, plain and definitive language, as they know their readers will best be able to understand this. Most press releases and announcements get very little publicity - they get deleted.

Chasing quotes

Journalists often ask dumb questions. We sometimes ask questions, even when we know what the answer is. This is because we are attempting to elicit a quote from an interviewee which we can then simply write into a story.

This might sound obvious. However, all too often, when I am interviewing someone over the phone or have sent over some questions by email, my questions elicit 'yes' or 'no' answers, or sentences that are so short they are effectively useless as a quote. On the other hand, I sometimes find myself sat with an interviewee who is so verbose that I dread to ask another question as I know this will lead to another interminably long answer.

Good quotes

Getting the balance right comes more naturally to some than it does to others. I recommend to anyone to regularly read a few stories in a newspaper and look at the quotes that made it into print.

You'll notice they have several things in common:

Most use plain English - not highly technical language or marketing speak

They cut to the chase, the people very quickly say what they mean in no uncertain terms; they express a point of view

They are not salesy. Journalists don't want to sell your product – they want to tell your story

They are of interest to the readers of the title.

Journalists are writing for their audiences. If it's a local paper, they'll be looking for comments and insight into their local area. So, when I wrote a press release about my business for the Brighton Argus (which was published in full), I added the following quotes:

"Brighton is a hot spot for media companies and has a very strong freelancer and small business community. We really want to see more companies from this city gain the coverage they deserve and come to national prominence.

"Brighton has produced some excellent companies, particularly in the digital and new technology spaces. We have some big names like Brandwatch but also some really interesting growing businesses like MakerClub, Dragon Bench and all the hot new start-ups at the Digital Catapult."

You can see from the quotes above that I really don't attempt to sell my company or services at all. Instead, I talk about the city, the industry and even other companies. This meant I was much more of a commentator and voice of the city, rather than simply an entrepreneur trying to get my name out there. But the story still referenced who we were, what we did and how we were trying to make a difference. In effect, this is a kind of sell, but in a much softer way.

Body copy

Now let's move on to what's the least important component for you - the body copy. It may surprise you that I think this is the least important but, as a journalist of 15 years, I can tell you that we are very good at writing and editing things. So, you don't need to obsess about the body copy of your press release, op-ed or story. You're not a professional writer and any work you send is likely (hopefully) to be edited.

But, if you are writing a story, you need to ask and answer key questions: who, what, where, why, when and how. It may surprise you but I really have received stories which omitted the following:

Person's name/company name (who)
Description of the company's activities (what)
Location of the business (where)
Interesting reason for the story (why)
Dates, times (when)
Details on the plans (how)

When key questions remain unanswered, we say: 'there are holes in the story'. Put in plenty of details into your stories, answer lots of questions. You can read more on this in the upcoming chapter: Writing the News.

Pictures

Pictures are one of the most neglected components of the media package, yet they are crucial. The first advice I always give to entrepreneurs is very simple:

"Get a photoshoot!"

But don't scrimp on photos.

Hiring a professional photographer isn't very expensive and it's worth spending a little more to get one with experience of working for the national media.

If you want your pictures to be published in the press then it stands to reason you need newspaper quality pictures. Therefore, you need a snapper whose work is regularly published in the outlets you want to be in. Finding these photographers is easy. Just check out the credits on the pictures of the business sections of the newspapers and Google them.

But don't just hire a photographer to take some boring headshots of you in a business suit. Spend some time thinking about the pictures and how they will work alongside the rest of the media package. Think about the headlines, the quotes, your story and the picture that will convey all of this to the reader.

An exciting picture really is the difference between get published or not.

Imagery defines the news agenda. Story selection is regularly determined by the quality of the pictures available.

I advise you to read through the business sections of national newspapers and look carefully at the pictures. It's very important you appreciate that all the larger features require high quality imagery and, unless that is available, a feature simply cannot run. But newspapers and magazines have limited budgets and can't afford to send a photographer out to every interviewee. Media savvy entrepreneurs always invest in photoshoots. Do you really think the likes of Branson, Jobs, Musk and Roddick did photoshoots on the cheap? Or that they simply wait for a newspaper to send out a photographer? Take control of your imagery.

You'll need to create professional, high resolution pictures that illustrate what you do. If you have physical products then find a way to include them into the shot. If you work in the aerospace industry then do a shoot near an airfield with planes as your backdrop.

I appreciate that many online businesses might struggle to think of ways to convey what they do in a single image. So, I recommend you think about the impact of your business on the world and what it means to your customers. Hopefully, this will trigger some ideas. Think long and hard about pictures and don't leave them until the last minute. See Chapter 8: Pictures, Pictures, Pictures, for more on this.

News Pegs

"It's a good story, Jon, but we need a peg to hang it on", a former news editor would say to me. Often, entrepreneurs tell me about something cool in their business or industry and don't understand why no-one is talking about it. Sometimes, the answer is because the story lacks a 'news peg'.

A news peg is what connects a story about your business with wider events. The peg could be the the World Cup, plastic in the ocean, or a storyline from a TV show. A journalist will cite this example and then talk about businesses that are connected to this story - pegging them together.

I was recently writing a piece about leadership for The Telegraph and my editor wanted a 'contemporary news angle'. The World Cup was on and the leadership of England's manager Gareth Southgate was a hot topic. So, I pegged the two together and wrote a piece with the headline 'How to create Gareth Southgate-style 'super teams''. The feature did well, gaining a lot of shares and views. It probably would have done even better had England not lost their next game.

Facts and Figures

A detailed news story will contain facts and figures to substantiate or rebuff the claims made in the story and give it more credence in the eyes of the reader. This is an area where many business owners can be of great service to journalists in sharing their knowledge and expertise and helping them to research a story.

Journalists tend to cover a wide range of topics and may lack the detailed knowledge held by some of their interviewees. Also, they are typically from humanities and arts backgrounds; more have BAs than BScs and so they aren't as scientifically minded as they might wish to be. So often, we rely on 'experts' to tell us things and point us in the right direction. Being a useful expert is a great role for a business owner and they tend to get rewarded in coverage. If you know a journalist is looking for information, sending them a useful link, PDF report or, indeed, an authoritative quote, is a great way to build a relationship with them.

If a company is the first, the fastest or the biggest or strongest, then this might be a good angle for the journalist to work upon. However, it is no good simply saying that this was the fastest crowdfunding from a UK company this year. Such claims need to be justified or corroborated by additional sources.

But many pertinent facts are to be found by asking those key questions: who, what, where, why when and how. Anticipating these will make you a better interviewee and source.

Links

It's always worth asking for a link and many publications do oblige. Make sure you know which page you want to be linked to and send that over to the journalist via email. The journalist may want to link their work to other pages containing facts and figures. Ultimately, that will be their decision, but it's always worth keeping in mind. See chapter 8: Getting Links for more on this somewhat controversial topic.

CHAPTER 3 EXERCISES

#1 Examine the headlines in the newspapers and magazines you'd like to appear in. What sort of verbs, nouns and adjectives do they use? Now create some headlines for your business.

#2 Be interviewed. Either find a journalist and beg/pay them to interview you, or ask a member of your team to ask you lots of questions and record your answers. Read over your quotes – are you happy with how you sound?

#3 Create a batch of quotes about your business, industry and main interests.

#4 Review the press releases and media dispatches you have sent out to date. Look at each of the components – headlines, quotes, pictures. Are they good enough for a journalist to use?

#5 Read the next chapter and then get a photoshoot.

PICTURES, PICTURES, PICTURES

One of my earliest jobs as a journalist involved covering major crimes - stabbings, sex crimes and murder. I interviewed victims and their families and wrote their stories. A minimum of two pictures were always required for these types of stories; the victim and the perpetrator. However, for a murder case, this was always a challenge, as the perpetrator was usually behind bars and the victim was, of course, no longer available. So, either pictures were available, and the feature could run, or they weren't, and it would be 'spiked'.

This macabre initiation into journalism helped me appreciate just how critical pictures are to how the media works. **If there are no pictures, there is no story.**

Thankfully, business journalists tend to have a little more wiggle room than those working the crime beat. However, pictures still play an absolutely vital role. Therefore, one of the first things I advise a company to do before it attempts to gain publicity is to **get a photoshoot.**

Newspapers and online publications operate on ever tighter margins. Most do not employ photographers directly and, those that do, such as the major national newspapers, also rely on freelance photographers and agencies for their pictures. Photography is a cost, and many commissioning editors simply do not have the budget to pay for a photographer to come and visit your business. Yet all journalists agree that pictures are crucial.

"I'd invest in good photography," says Emma Sheppard, content co-ordinator at the Guardian. "We don't often have the budget to send a photographer anymore. But if you have great photos of your business, yourself, your products and your shop, we're more likely to feature you. Especially if we're doing a gallery."

"Pictures are very important," agrees Dan Matthews, editor of MinuteHack and freelance journalist for The Daily Telegraph, The Guardian and Forbes. "I am part-time editor of two mags, one with a large picture budget and one with stock only - the difference is clear."

With newspapers' budgets so painfully tight, it is essential for entrepreneurs attempting to do their own PR to have a good selection of high resolution, professional, interesting and illustrative pictures.

I often write stories about exciting entrepreneurs who have embarked on great endeavours destined to shake up an industry and bring in riches. I usually request a picture of my interviewee and what comes back is quite often a headshot of a middle-aged man wearing a grey suit. Business owners need to get more creative.

Rebecca Burn-Callander is a freelance business journalist and former enterprise editor at the Telegraph. She has commissioned photoshoots but says it's generally better when they've been done in advance. "Newspapers will shoot stories if they have to, but it is a massive win if you have them already, because a great picture can help the journalist pitch the story in the first place. Try and get a variety – never just 'man in suit behind desk'. You want colour and energy," she says.

All big stories need a picture to go alongside them and a good photoshoot does not need to cost a huge amount of money. A photographer with a good portfolio and experience working for newspapers and magazines can be hired for the day for a few hundred pounds.

However, prior to booking a photoshoot, it's a good idea to think about what the end result will be. This might mean finding props or choosing a location that says something about the business. If you have physical products then bring them to the shoot. If not, think of something you can use that will make the picture more interesting.

The business sections of the Times and Sunday Times are often good places to look for inspiration. They regularly contain stories about entrepreneurs and good quality photography is highly valued by the newspaper group.

"For enterprise-led stories, we're particularly looking for pictures that will help tell the story," says James Hurley, enterprise editor at The Times. "A good business section is always looking for lively pictures that are not a load of blokes in suits. A good picture can bring the pages, and a story, to life."

Case study: Photoshoot on a shoestring

A few years ago, I was writing a piece for the Guardian newspaper. My brief was to speak to three business owners, write 500 words about each and ask them to send a picture of themselves to the Guardian's picture desk. One of the entrepreneurs asked my advice on what sort of picture I thought would be suitable to send to the newspaper. He didn't have much money and we needed the pictures fairly soon. Here's what I told him:

"Make yourself look smart - have a shave, comb your hair and dress smartly. Find a friend with a decent camera as you'll need a high resolution picture. It should definitely be a couple of megabytes. I suggest you take the picture outside, as natural light will improve the result. But also, I suggest that you keep your product in the shot. An illustrative picture is always a good idea."

The entrepreneur did exactly as I told him and, to my pleasure and surprise, his story was placed highest on the page, alongside his picture. The other two entrepreneurs, who had not asked my advice, sent across pictures which were not as good in the eyes of the picture editor.

As the journalists above have suggested, nobody wants another picture of a 'man in a suit'. But nonetheless, I do recommend business owners dress well for a photoshoot. It's generally better to be overdressed for a photoshoot than underdressed, so that you don't end up looking like a scruff. If you're the leader of your company, good clothing will bring a sense of gravitas. However, the key is to ensure your pictures are illustrative of what you do.

Getting the resolution right

One thing which is non-negotiable is having a high-resolution picture. A picture that is too small simply cannot be blown up by a designer laying out a page. Low-resolution images really can lead to entrepreneurs getting less coverage than those that send high-res images.

Most of us have pictures of ourselves on mobile phones. While this can be useful, it can also lead to bad habits. I recently interviewed the chief financial officer of a large business for a feature in a national newspaper. As is the norm, I requested a photograph of my interviewee. However, the picture he sent was shot on a camera phone. The file was a mere 300 kilobytes, making it far too small. Thankfully, the publication's design team were able to use a few effects to mask the fact that the picture was low resolution. The story went ahead. However, it came painfully close to being cut.

Group shots

You'll also notice when looking at the pictures in a national newspaper that there are very few group shots; most pictures contain just one person per shot. Generally, if a story quotes just one person, the picture will be of that person. Many picture editors hate group shots – 'save them for the community newsletter'.

THE PHOTOGRAPHER'S VIEW

Andrew Hasson has worked as a photographer for the international press for over 30 years. His work appears regularly in titles including the Sunday Times, Daily Telegraph and Guardian. Here, Andrew explains what entrepreneurs need to know about photoshoots.

"Picture editors want something that makes their publication look great – different, exciting and colourful," says Andrew Hasson, who has taken many calls from picture editors on a deadline. "They want something that makes the reader think: 'Ooh, that looks interesting; I wonder what's going on there?'"

Photography is critical to the success of all publications. If a title doesn't look good then readers aren't going to buy it or read it. Those in charge of selecting pictures have to find the right images to entice people to read the story.

Tight newspaper budgets mean that there are far fewer direct commissions for photographers now than there were a decade or so ago. Realistically, businesses that achieve significant coverage have invested in their own photoshoots, rather than relying on a newspaper to send out a snapper.

Hasson is often engaged directly by businesses who later provide his pictures to the titles themselves. But this shift means it is crucial entrepreneurs understand the basics of a successful shoot, so they can work with a professional to get the right results.

"Pictures are critical. Can you imagine reading the business pages where there wasn't a single picture? A strong, engaging set of pictures will always take precedence over a boring headshot."

Good pictures take time. The scene needs be set, the right poses and expressions found, and lighting and weather play a part, too – you can't rush a good photo. "Leave enough time for yourself. Don't try and crowbar a photoshoot in between two important business meetings. The pressure will show in the photos," warns Hasson.

Dressing and grooming well is important. Generally, black and white clothing are to be avoided, "unless it's really your thing". Primary colours, red in particular, stand out against the black and white of a newspaper or web page.

The photographer can only guide you – they don't control you. Nerves and a degree of self-consciousness are normal. "Accept this as part and parcel of your business. Be professional about it. Photoshoots can be fun and exciting and will help your business, so embrace them. Don't start by telling the photographer you hate having your picture taken or don't really see the point."

The best results are often created outside – there's no light better than the sun. An attractive setting is helpful, too. "A blank background, or leaning up against a brick wall, rarely work unless the subject really knows what they're doing."

The photographer will know when he's got his best shots of you and you'll need to keep working until he has them. Hasson loves to see his work published in top tier titles, it's personally satisfying and good for his reputation.

"Every newspaper and magazine editor wants their product to look brilliant and will accept with open arms a photo that helps achieve that aim. This means a great photo can really make a difference if you're aiming to gain publicity for your business. So, keep working until you get the right result – it's very satisfying when you do. Only look at your watch when the photographer tells you they are finished."

CHAPTER 4 EXERCISES

#1 Take a look at any photos you've previously sent to the press. Were they professional, high resolution and illustrative?

#2 Start to plan your photoshoot. Look at the pictures in your desired newspapers and magazines for inspiration.

#3 Seek out the right photographer for you. I strongly recommend someone with experience of working with the national media.

#4 Get a photoshoot!

CHAPTER 5

JOURNALIST REQUESTS

Very often, I receive an email from a PR which reads something like this: "Hi Jon, loved your piece in the Telegraph about Blockchain. Perhaps you'd be interested in talking to my client, who's doing great things in the Blockchain space."

I don't usually respond, but what I'd like to say is this: "Yes, I did write a feature about that and maybe your client would have been great. But it's too late. The feature has been written. That ship has sailed and I'm unlikely to be writing a piece about that very same subject anytime soon, at least, not for The Telegraph."

People often ask me: 'when is the best time to contact a journalist?' To which, I reply: 'when they are writing a story where you'd be a relevant interviewee'. My reply is not meant to sound trite. Rather, I am referring to the fact that journalists are now advertising the fact that they are writing specific stories and encouraging people to pitch themselves as potential interviewees.

Journalist requests

The digital age has brought with it an entirely new model for getting press for your business. In the past, companies needed to build a rapport with key journalists, or pay an agency to do so on their behalf. However, digital technology can now be used by entrepreneurs and business owners to connect with the media and allow them to obtain top tier coverage, in minutes, regardless of their size.

Systems like #journorequest, HARO and Response Source present excellent opportunities for new businesses to get in direct contact with journalists. Journalists use these hashtags and services to release shout outs and encourage entrepreneurs to drop them a line.

"I think, for businesses in particular, journalists are much easier to reach now, thanks to Twitter, but also sites such as Response Source and Journolink. We're always looking for case studies, often on quite a short deadline, and this broadens our network very quickly," says The Guardian's Emma Sheppard.

Writers and editors from all of the world's most well-known news outlets are now using journalist requests to find case studies, boost their contacts and get those crucial components for their stories. Any entrepreneur interested in gaining press and publicity must be aware of this method of getting press.

My wife Corinne is a veritable expert of journalist requests. She honed her skills getting press for Andy Atalla, founder of digital agency atom42. Andy appeared in the Financial Times, Guardian, BBC and many other places. But she's since gained clients coverage in titles all across the world, including every British newspaper and major broadcaster.

Here, she gives an overview of the main journalist request services to check out. Some are free but the paid ones might very well be worth it, too.

#journorequest

The #journorequest hashtag is now an established system for journalists to request expert opinions and other contributions via Twitter. Just follow the hashtag and you'll find a stream of regular media opportunities you can get involved with, free of charge. But bear in mind, the brilliant simplicity of this can also be its drawback, as popular journalist requests will lead to an inundation of responses - competition is high. Also, the length of a Tweet - 280 characters - doesn't allow for a huge amount of detail about what the journalist is after. This makes it difficult for businesses to know if they're offering something that's really going to be useful. But it's free, so why not give it a go?

Key tip: You have to be super-fast with #journorequest, so remember to press the 'Latest' tab - Twitter defaults to 'Top'.

HARO (Help a Reporter Out)

Sign up to this email digest and you'll gain access to another free stream of regular media opportunities, though the majority on HARO are for US publications. And, again, the fact that it's free can make it highly competitive. You can pay a fee to receive these requests slightly earlier. A speedy response is a major plus when it comes to journalist requests - journalists are always on a deadline - so consider paying for the early access if you think you can reply to the requests very quickly. The information available via the HARO email is slightly more detailed than the #journorequest hashtag requests, meaning you're more likely to give them what they want.

Response Source

Over the years, we've had by far the most success with Response Source. For Jon, this has been in terms of gaining the best sources for articles, and for clients, in getting press. While it does require an investment for anything more than the one-week trial, the opportunities are often high level and the competition is much lower than with the free options. Plus, the form journalists are required to fill in, including a reasonably detailed description of what they're looking for, offers businesses much more chance to find out, and give them, exactly what they're looking for.

Response Source can be a good investment for your business. Look through the categories they offer and ask to trial all the topics which seem relevant to your business. Then take the free trial and see what kinds of opportunities come up.

JournoLink

A relative newcomer to the media request pack, JournoLink was launched in 2014 and is designed to offer small businesses an affordable media package. You can choose a monthly or annual subscription to receive journalist requests and distribute press releases, as well as building a profile which can be found by journalists looking for a case study. Worth checking out with the free trial.

Taking the journalist's perspective

Journalists have got a job to do - they're on a deadline to produce an article, perhaps of some complexity. They send out a request and hope the information they need to make the article work comes back to them. If they get three responses in the first hour, offering enough information for their article, they might start to put it together then and there, at least in their mind's eye. They might mentally adjust the angle of the article, so those three contributors make sense in context. It's human nature to try and make sense of a complex topic, and come to a satisfying conclusion, as quickly as we can. Whatever deadline a journalist has written down for respondents, it's possible that the article will be all but written within a few hours.

I've even seen articles being published within two hours of the request being sent. So, if you can be first, and reply within the hour with exactly what the journalist wants, you have a much higher chance of getting noticed, and getting press.

When should you answer?

While you will want to respond to plenty of requests, you'll always need to read the request carefully and decide if the article is likely to be right for you. You need to be a genuinely good source for the journalist. You should never pretend to be something you're not. However, you'll sometimes want to think laterally about the question the journalist is asking and what you could offer their readers. For example, you might be able to provide a new or surprising angle on a topic, due to your field of expertise, even if it's not your core business offering.

Next, consider if the particular media opportunity is right for you and worth the effort of replying. Usually, if something's relevant, it makes sense to at least have a go. But if you get the sense that the article or publisher is completely at odds with your company values, it makes sense to give it a miss. If you have decided the topic is relevant and you want to contribute, this is when the fun begins. "If you can reply with exactly what the journalist wants, you could well just hit the jackpot with a brilliant bit of media coverage, worth thousands of pounds to your business," says Corinne.

Time is of the essence

Journalists often receive a huge number of replies to their requests. When I'm writing about a topic for a national newspaper, I can receive over 100 replies, which can pour into my inbox in just a few hours. My own experience, and that of other journalists, shows that the replies which come in first have a better chance of being used than those that come later.

"If at all possible, reply quickly, and ideally within the hour. If you can't do this, it doesn't rule you out, but your response is more likely to get lost among the higher number of latecomers to the journalist request," says Corinne.

Killer intros

To make a great impression with your replies, you'll want to send a killer one or two-sentence intro about yourself and your business. This killer intro needs sell you and your business, fast and effectively. It needs to succinctly define who you are and explain why you'd be perfect for an interview.

It should say what your business does, mention some well-known clients, awards and any other achievements or details that give you credibility. It should be written in the third person – this way it can be published directly ahead of your quote. You can then tweak your intro slightly if necessary, depending on the topic of the request.

Here are some examples of genuine and effective killer intros:

Sophie Devonshire is CEO at strategic consultancy The Caffeine Partnership, advising leaders at Fortune 500 companies including Nissan, L'Oreal and Unilever.

She is the author of 'Superfast: Lead at Speed', in which she interviews 100 of the world's foremost business executives and entrepreneurs from companies such as Google, Farfetch and Innocent Drinks.

What makes these sentences killer?

Sophie is the CEO therefore the head of the business. Journalists want to speak to 'the boss' so founders, CEOs and managing directors are best. In two words, the business is defined: 'strategic consultancy'. Journalists like brevity. The credibility of both Sophie's business and her book is defined by her well-known clients and interviewees. Here, we use the 'law of threes' – three big client names to convince you this is a respected entrepreneur.

Christine Telyan is CEO and co-founder of London-based tech company UENI, which builds over 3000 websites per day. The company has raised over £15m in angel investment and is active in the UK, Spain, France, India, and the United States.

What makes these sentences killer?

Christine is also the CEO but her business doesn't have big name clients, therefore we instead use numbers to denote success; 3000 websites, £15m in investment. We also refer to the company's international expansion.

Jon Card is the co-founder of media training company Full Story Media and has worked as a business journalist for The Guardian, Daily Telegraph and The Times. He is a public speaker and has delivered lectures and workshops for business audiences at The Supper Club, UK Trade Investment and Clean and Cool.

What makes these sentences killer?

Ok, so this is me, and my big plays are the newspapers I write for. Again, this is the 'Law of Threes' in action. You only need three big names - four is overkill.

Quotes and commentary

When a journalist is writing a story, one of the key parts of the package is quotes. So, after you've introduced yourself or your client with a killer intro, why not get the ball rolling with a killer quote?

I've already covered quotes in a previous chapter but, when responding to a journalist request, you have a real opportunity to get into the mindset of the journalist and, crucially, their readership. Within the request there will be key information to guide you.

Beyond that, it is usually fairly straightforward to work out the type of stories the journalist specialises in. A quick Google of 'Jon Card' reveals that I mostly write about business and enterprise. My Twitter and LinkedIn profile will tell you more.

So, before you respond, do your best to ascertain who this journalist is, what publication they are writing for and who the readership is likely to be.

Quotes are such an important part of the package and really do determine who gets included in the piece and who doesn't. Try to give the readership something useful, insightful and authoritative. People who are great at providing commentary are good at expressing a point of view – don't equivocate, call it as you see it and don't be afraid to demonstrate your expertise and knowledge.

CHAPTER 5 EXERCISES

#1 Work on some killer sentences about yourself, similar to those in this section. Define yourself succinctly with credibility and authority.

#2 Try out #journorequest, HARO, Response Source and JournoLink.

WRITING THE NEWS

Journalism is in decline and there are simply fewer journalists working in newsrooms to meet the public's hungry demand for stories. In one sense, there has never been more demand for the work of journalists; we consume more news and information than ever. But there is precious little money to pay for the work of journalists and no decent business model to attract it. In the digital age, content is largely free and advertising money doesn't come close to paying for the type of journalism we really need.

But this book isn't a whinge about the state of the British or global media. Rather, it is to offer entrepreneurs a route to engaging with the press and use it to their advantage. Entrepreneurs need to become storytellers if they are to engage and interest journalists. But, increasingly, they need to get into the content game and start writing and producing their own stories.

This chapter could have been called: 'how to write a press release'. But that would have given you entirely the wrong idea. Because, while companies think they need to 'send out a press release', what they really need to do is to write stories.

In the past, PRs would send out very formal press releases, written in rather peculiar ways, and a journalist would have taken parts to use in their stories. But as journalist numbers declined, whole stories started to be written from press releases, particularly as online media took hold. In today's lightning-paced digital world, the way a story is written has become a determining factor in what gets published. In some editorial teams, journalists are hammering out news stories from press releases all day long. It makes sense to send them something which is pretty much 'oven ready'.

Stories are 'packages'; a collection of components the journalist must assemble before they can publish. But now we need to think about the sorts of stories that really turn our heads. Journalists develop news antennae. We learn to spot a good story from a distance. It's something I'm very good at - spotting a story has always been my superpower. But I believe it's a learnable skill and can be of great benefit to storytelling entrepreneurs.

Is there really a story?

The first thing you need to do is to decide is if you actually have something which is worth writing about. Is there really a story there? Far too many press releases are sent out when, in fact, there isn't much to say. It doesn't take much to get journalists to open up about this issue.

"Don't get in touch with a journalist if your message is just: 'please write about me'," says Madeleine Cuff, deputy editor of BusinessGreen. "Journalists are massively time pressed and we get literally hundreds of calls and emails a week. We're unlikely to listen unless you have thought carefully about why your story should be told now, and why it's relevant for our readers." Madeleine expresses a point made regularly by journalists as they peruse their inboxes scanning over scores of press releases: most lack any real substance. Also, she wants a story that is both relevant to her readers and not overly promotional.

"I like stories that surprise me," says Rebecca Burn-Callander, freelance business journalist and former enterprise editor for the Telegraph. "Things that I want to tell my friends about at the pub on the weekend in a conversation that starts: "You'll never guess...". There is nothing worse than a survey that tells you nothing new, like 99pc of people don't like Mondays. Big woo."

As Rebecca says, a good story is one you want to repeat. Often, they do contain surprise elements. Many newspaper headlines contain a juxtaposition. They take two things that don't really fit together and place them side by side. For instance, my friend Caspar Craven has sailed around the world:

BRITISH MAN SAILS AROUND THE WORLD

Well, big deal. Humans have been doing that for hundreds of years. But let's add a surprise element:

SAILING AROUND THE WORLD WITH THREE CHILDREN

This headline, which appeared on CNN, contains that surprise element. A big, strong man like Caspar sailing around the world isn't that exciting, but add three kids clutching to his ankles and we've got a story Rebecca wants to tell her mates in the pub. We don't expect to see toddlers and primary school kids in the middle of the Pacific Ocean. But that's what happened and, yes, there are also some marvellous pictures.

Stories in the business world aren't always quite as dramatic but they can still contain surprise and juxtaposition.

The following headline is fairly mediocre:

MICROSOFT INVESTS £5M IN HOTEL BOOKING COMPANY

However, adding some surprise and juxtaposition changes it completely as the below example shows:

MICROSOFT INVESTS £5M IN START-UP FOUNDED BY HOTEL PORTER

Some stories use quotes in the headline such as:

"I used to carry cases for Bill Gates, now he's bought my company."

Stories are about people

Stories are about people, not technology, products, services or results. If you've just completed a big deal, you should tell us how this will affect you, your staff and other people. Perhaps the '£2m deal' will mean the creation of 10 new jobs? Stories need to have a human element to them.

As Guardian journalist Emma Sheppard says:
"I'm interested in the people behind the story.
"I'm looking for a unique angle. Something that makes you sit up and take notice."

Emma has written many stories for The Guardian. One that caught my eye was entitled: 'Young Entrepreneurs in Syria: they'll rebuild what the war has destroyed'. The contrast of a start-up entrepreneur and a warzone is clear and just the sort of thing that would make the journalist's news antennae beep.

Good stories contain surprises, twists and turns and intrigue. But a journalist also needs to focus in on one part and create an angle. The angle informs the headline. So the £2m deal might become 'Fifty jobs saved by £2m rescue deal'.

But such stories, while perfectly newsworthy, are quite common and, in an age of technological marvels, journalists are looking for truly remarkable things to write about.

Crafting a story

Assuming you have a genuine story to tell, how exactly do you craft a press release? I tend to recommend to most entrepreneurs that they find someone with literary skills to help them, as even professional writers need a sub-editor. But here are some key provisos to follow when writing a story.

THE INVERTED PYRAMID: HOW TO STRUCTURE A NEWS STORY

News stories are inverted pyramids - the interesting stuff goes at the top, with the leftovers tacked on the bottom.

1# HEADLINE

It starts with a headline, arguably the most important part of the story, which is why it gets the widest part of the pyramid. The lettering is emboldened and may be in title case or a larger font. Headlines don't need to be long, though. Concise headlines usually work best in print, while slightly longer ones can work online. Remember: the words of headlines are simple, recognisable, evocative: 'famous'.

#2 THE STANDFIRST

Offering a little more description of the story, the standfirst must still replicate the theme of the headline. But it must not use the same words.

#3 FIRST PARAGRAPHS

The first few paragraphs of the body copy are busy. They are packed full of facts about the story. Every story is slightly different but, by the end of the first two to three paragraphs, you should have answered most of the main 'five Ws': Who, What, Why, Where, When.

#4 QUOTES

After the first couple of paragraphs come the quotes. You may have introduced the quoted person already, but you'll want to elaborate slightly on who they are before we hear them speak. There's no exact limit to the number of quotes you add, but I tend to recommend two to three sentences near the top and more later.

#5 MORE BODY

The remainder of the body copy should contain any other pertinent facts and figures, including the names of other people and places who are relevant to the story. I often intersperse these paragraphs with relevant quotes as I like my stories to be quite quote heavy. For press releases, more quotes means the journalist has more to choose from.

#6 FINAL DETAILS

At the bottom, there will be details that could reasonably be cut without it affecting the core of the story. Perhaps historical details on the story or quotes from other, less crucial commentators.

#7 NOTES TO EDITORS

These will not be published and tend to include additional company information and contact details.

Experts

Journalists love a scoop and, sometimes, the work of one reporter can set the news agenda. Newspapers never own a story for long as, soon, all of the other titles will be clamouring for a piece of the action. Suddenly journalists, with little prior knowledge of the story, are being asked to write pieces. They need someone to talk to; they need an expert.

The Cambridge Analytica scandal of 2018 led to a big demand for 'experts' on Facebook. Many analysts and advisors were propelled into the media spotlight to give their views on what all of this meant. Among them was Marie Page.

Already a published author, trainer and public speaker, Marie had opinions on the topic of Facebook and the knowledge to make them noteworthy. With her expert bio, high resolution photos and confidence to speak on all things Facebook, she soon became the journalists' go to spokesperson. She ended up speaking to top shows like ITV's Tonight programme and national titles like The Times and the Daily Express.

Most of Marie's appearances came as a result of responding to journalist requests. Corinne and I simply sent over her 'killer sentences', which she had drafted, and a few quotes.

Fortunately, Marie had a catalogue of successes and noteworthy achievements to give her words on the topic of Facebook power and credibility. Here's the extensive bio we dipped into when communicating with journalists on Marie's behalf:

Marie Page is a founding partner of digital marketing consultancy The Digiterati and the principle Facebook marketing instructor for Digiterati Academy, the online learning community for marketers and entrepreneurs. Her book 'Winning at Facebook Marketing with Zero Budget' is an Amazon bestseller. Marie's work on the Facebook News Feed algorithm was featured in The Huffington Post. Marie is a regular guest on digital marketing blogs and podcasts including Social Media Examiner and Smart Insights.

On top of a tailored, powerful intro taken from the bio above, Marie's quotes for the media pulled no punches. They had to be as strong as the headlines.

In an article for the Express titled: 'Facebook stock PLUMMETS as scrutiny intensifies'

Marie's contribution, for which she was introduced as 'One of the UK's leading Facebook marketing authorities', included a number of emotive statements such as:

"Facebook is the drug we can't do without".

"Users have short memories and their fear of missing out by deleting Facebook will soon overcome their concerns."

In her dealings with the media, Marie stood out. Not just for her credibility, but also for her willingness to provide a strong and grounded opinion, expressed with clarity and panache, that would be interesting to readers of the title in question. That's how you become a go-to expert in your field.

Your bio doesn't need to be as long and detailed as Marie's - a sentence or two will do - but you do need something that's powerful and expressed in a way that people outside your industry can easily understand.

Pick out the things you and your business have achieved, which are most likely to impress a journalist, giving them, and their readers, reasons to believe you are an expert in your field. These successes will form the introduction to any responses you provide to journalist requests.

Aligning your brand with national events

With the likes of Twitter infiltrating more and more of our daily lives, awareness days and national events are constantly pored over and at the front of people's minds. Your business can align itself with these events, building media opportunities out of otherwise less relevant events in your business's growth.

When Bristol-based tech entrepreneur Rav Bumbra was launching a new app to help women find the mentors they needed to get ahead in the tech business, she strategically planned the launch date to coincide with International Women's Day. This led to a list of media mentions including the Evening Standard, Cash Lady, We Are the City, MinuteHack and the Bristol Post.

Create a forward features calendar

If you can deliberately synchronize company events with relevant awareness days and weeks, as Rav did so effectively, this will help you get press for those events. But depending on your PR resources, you might choose to go further into the arena of awareness events. The best way to do this is to have a plan well in advance of those dates.

Many sites will show you upcoming events and awareness days, so you can work out when to target journalists with relevant content. Look ahead at these events and highlight any that chime with your brand's offering or values.

Build your plan for the year based on these awareness days and recurring events, then think of inventive ways you can provide something useful to the press, bloggers and influencers immediately before those dates that they can use for content, weaving your company in naturally at the same time.

Use your own experience, expertise and resources from within your company, to make this content both useful for the reader and low cost to you.

Be a pro newsjacker

While your forward features calendar will help you raise your press planning game to that of most PR professionals, a good way to get ahead of the PR competition is to look for the upcoming events that other people might not have spotted.

To do this, you need to know the press around your industry, and the press around your consumers' needs and interests, inside out.

As well as spying upcoming events, you might be able to jump on current events faster and more effectively than your competitors. Again, this will come with being constantly alert to events in and around your industry and how they relate to your audiences.

Key lessons

The digital revolution has levelled the playing field when it comes to getting media coverage for your business. Even as a small company, and without any established media connections, you can present yourself as an expert and gain top tier media coverage in the process. With the right tools and skills, it's possible to propel your business into the limelight, with little or no monetary cost.

CHAPTER 6 EXERCISES

#1 Is there anything extreme, unusual or exciting about your company? Biggest? Fastest? Oldest? First to market? Can these claims be proven?

#2 Try writing a news story about your business, based on what you've learned.

#3 Build a forward features calendar, including awareness dates and known industry events as well as any upcoming dates others might not have noticed, which you could prepare content around.

CHAPTER 7

LET'S GET DIGITAL

I started working as a journalist way back in 2002 and it's been a remarkable time. The digital revolution has transformed journalism so much since then. The internet and digital technologies were very much a part of newsrooms then, but there was very little in the way of social media; the biggest social network at the time was a site called Friends Reunited. Google was around, but people were still questioning whether or not it was the best search engine to use. Mobile phones were not particularly smart and they didn't have apps – the Apple App store launched in 2008 – and most didn't have cameras or, at least, not very good ones.

There were even some people who questioned whether or not the internet was here to stay – though this group was rapidly in decline.

Prior to the internet, the main job of journalists was to write. Their copy would then be passed through a series of editors and sub-editors, it would be designed and laid out, pictures would be added and the article would then enter the printing process.

The journalist's role today

Journalists don't merely write stories in the online age. One of the things that I am always keen to point out to young journalists, and anyone attending one of my media training sessions, is that writing is the easy bit.

Online journalists must assemble a story in a content management system (CMS). They must choose headlines and teasers and add tags, pictures, links and pull quotes. They're not just responsible for writing stories, but also for publishing, promoting and distributing them. Journalists, particularly freelance journalists such as myself, have to think more promotionally, tactically, indeed, more entrepreneurially. Journalists are often very aware and tuned into the work of marketers - appreciating concepts such as search engine optimisation (SEO) and the power of keywords - the terms that people might type into search engines which could result in them reading your article.

As journalist and editor Rebecca Burn-Callander says, the role of a journalist in the digital age is now very different from what it was a few years ago.

"The digital revolution completely changed my job. In the early days, I just had to find and research and write stories," Rebecca says. "Suddenly, I was finding, researching, writing stories, then finding pictures, uploading them to a CMS, placing stories on the right landing page, putting in links, adding the right SEO tags, inserting pictures and tagging those for SEO, adding sub heads, posting on social media and dealing with comments."

Media savvy entrepreneurs and PRs recognise these shifts and adapt their own strategies accordingly. Journalists want their stories to do well; they want them to be read by large numbers of people and to have some sort of influence. Furthermore, their efforts are being monitored and measured in terms of web traffic and social media shares.

This is something that many in the PR industry have not fully taken on board. From a PR perspective, it makes sense not only help journalists to write their stories and ensure that they get published, but also to ally yourself with them as they promote and distribute those stories across social media. By doing this, you'll increase the influence of your contribution to the article. But you'll also make friends with any journalists you're dealing with, who'll be delighted by the extra reach you're generating on their behalf.

Another aspect of this digital world is that online news articles can provide more than publicity. With a bit of extra planning, articles published online can also improve your digital authority in the eyes of the search engines. This is because news sites can, in certain circumstances, provide businesses with valuable inbound links. A delicate topic which we're about to unravel.

Links

So you've bagged an interview and told a journalist your story. They've indicated they want to publish your piece. But what you'd really like is for there to be a link from the story to your website.

With the rise of digital PR and more and more businesses understanding the basics of search engine optimisation (SEO), many publishers feel under siege with the number of people asking them to add links to their clients' or their own company's websites.

Often, journalists will have to turn down a request. This makes for an awkward interaction on both sides, but the fact remains that a link from a news site is a precious thing. Many would consider a link from a national newspaper as 'SEO gold'. I've witnessed a blue-chip company hire a PR agency for a six-figure fee, with a specific remit of conquering one of SEO's holy grails: a link from the BBC.

This chapter gives ideas on how to get a link included, both from the digital PR's perspective, and from that of the journalist.

Why get an inbound link included in your story?

If you don't know why a link might be valuable, it all has to do with the nature of the internet, where search algorithms like Google's have historically treated hyperlinks as 'votes' for a website.

The more authoritative links pointing to a particular site, the more that company's website will be able to rank for relevant search terms - the terms people type into Google – and the more likely they are to be found by new customers.

National news sites like the BBC are some of most authoritative sites on the internet, meaning an inbound link from a big news site is a huge win for any company.

With consumers now looking online as a first port of call to research products before buying them, online visibility is often a deciding factor in a company's success. Hence the incessant clamouring for high value links - and the resulting tension between marketers and journalists.

How do I get a link to my site included in a news article?

Getting a link can depend on the editorial policy and the whims of the journalist posting.

While links should be useful to the reader, there are instances in which a journalist will include a link to a website without the need for a separate piece of useful content on that site. As long the link still makes some sense in context, it is possible to get a simple homepage link into the article.

For example, where a company has provided a quote, a journalist might choose to include the link back to the company's website.

As a journalist, I tend to send website links to my editors along with my articles, and titles like The Guardian and Telegraph are quite reasonable about linking. Some are less so....

As an interviewee, you might be more persuasive than a PR. But always think about quid pro quo.

Journalists want their stories to be read and often get judged in terms of shares and links. If you have a strong network, ensure they know about it and that you will share their stories with your followers. Also, continue to be that useful, friendly expert that helps the journalist write their stories. This will give you more influence, with more chance of getting what you want, be it links or anything else.

What else can you do to get a link?

Beyond being helpful and friendly, there is more you can do to increase your chances of getting a link included in a news article. For a large number of publications, they'll need something called: 'editorial justification'.

They need to be able to justify the link from the perspective of their typical reader. You can do this by providing something useful or interesting on your site, that's not available in any press release that you send out. Or, give the reader something to do on your site, like enter a competition, or register for something they'll value.

Examples of a justifiable inbound link:
A link to a site where you can donate to a crowdfunder, where the article mentions that crowdfunder

A link to a site where the reader can enter a live competition, where the competition is still open for entries

A link to a site where you can find more details of a ground-breaking report on the topic in the article

Links that journalists usually remove:
A link to a site or page that's not relevant to the story

A link which is clearly promotional in nature

A number of links, all connected with one company - just choose the one that's most relevant for the reader

Email interviews

A lot of the interaction that you'll have with a journalist will be via email or messenger services. Journalists still use telephones, but they are increasingly hard to contact that way.

"I have more or less stopped answering my landline at certain times of the day because of the constant bombardment, 90 per cent of which is for stuff that is not usable or downright irrelevant. It's a shame because it does mean I miss some good ideas," says James Hurley, enterprise editor at The Times.

But as journalists ignore their phones, their email inboxes have taken the heat. On an average day, I receive over 100 emails - and many of my colleagues receive over 1,000.

Well written emails and stories are a must if you want to succeed in today's media. Journalists are also increasingly conducting interviews via email, preferring to send out written questions rather than conducting interviews over the phone.

If you receive a list of questions from a journalist, it is important to remember that they are attempting to elicit quotes from you. Avoid answering questions with a 'yes' or 'no' - even if they are closed questions. Instead, aim to answer each question with a few meaningful sentences.

There are many downsides to conducting an interview by email, most notably the lack of rapport between interviewer and interviewee. But there are substantial advantages, too. From the journalist's perspective, it is faster and less risky - a disgruntled interviewee can't dispute a quote sent by email. However, as an interviewee, it is important that you check your own quotes before you send them.

Finally, one reflection on the impact of digital on journalism:

Many of the quotes you read in a newspaper have never been spoken by anyone, they were only ever written.

CHAPTER 7 EXERCISES

#1 Think of three ways you could encourage journalists to link to your website from their publication.

#2 Consider the content on your website. How useful is it?

#3 If a journalist wanted to use you as a source, how could you help them? What are you expert in? What insider knowledge do you possess?

UNDERSTANDING JOURNALISTS

Journalists in the 21ˢᵗ century find themselves in a precarious position. Their numbers are falling, titles are closing and publishers are cutting back on their editorial budgets. Entrepreneurs need to appreciate that journalists are short on time and budgets and that their attention and focus are, all too often, being interrupted.

There's a general consensus across the media industry that journalism is in decline; jobs are fewer, salaries are poor and publishers are struggling. However, it is harder to say that there are simply fewer journalists in the UK today.

There are estimated to be around 73,000 journalists in the UK, according to figures from the Labour Force Survey (LFS) 2017. However, the LFS survey's figures vary greatly from year to year, for a variety of reasons. Definition is one problem. Unlike many occupations, journalists don't require formal qualifications and, thus, the title 'journalist' is something one adopts, rather than one which is bestowed. Also, the number of journalists tends to be inflated by the numbers of freelancers, part-timers and second-jobbers.

Many journalists regularly engage in non-journalistic activity – copywriting, blogging, consultancy, training, PR and other writing – this is my experience and that of many of my colleagues. Indeed, the Labour Force Survey estimated that 20,000 of the 73,000 "journalists" in the UK were freelance and we freelancers go where the money is.

Industry in decline

There is no doubt that the number of journalists employed by newspapers and magazines has declined substantially since the 1990s - the local press has shrunk dramatically. In 2015, Press Gazette estimated that the number of professional journalists employed in the local press had fallen by half since before 2008. Other studies have shown similar declines in both the numbers employed and the number of titles in operation.

Meanwhile, the UK's national titles are making a loss and seeking efficiencies:

The Guardian Media Group, which owns the Guardian and Observer titles, made losses of £45m in the financial year ending in April 2017. During that year it cut its staff numbers by around 300.

Rupert Murdoch's News Corp made losses of £629m in 2017. Murdoch owns UK titles such as The Sun (losses £24m) The Times (losses £6.5m). Both of these titles have also seen redundancies and cuts to editorial budgets.

Finally, an independent review: 'Tackling the threat to high-quality journalism in the UK', published on the gov.uk website on June 28th 2018, revealed that:

Total press industry revenues had declined by more than half over the last ten years

The number of full-time journalists had fallen by over 25% since 2007

- *A quarter of all regional and local newspapers had closed in the past decade*

The business model

It has long been my view that the business models of most publishers, which is primarily based on advertising and sponsorship, is not fit for purpose. Revenues from online advertising are substantially lower than from print although, in truth, advertising as a way to fund editorial has always been problematic.

Advertisers to the mass market need their numbers. But good editorial and investigative journalism doesn't always equate to large readerships. Readers often prefer to be entertained by celebrity gossip, rather than to focus on serious matters of public interest. Until its closure in 2011, the biggest selling newspaper in Europe was the News of the World.

Publishers struggle to fund large editorial teams and have little financial incentive to do so. But they do need content. This can, all too often, lead to a focus on quantity, rather than quality. It can also lead to an emphasis on speed, rather than accuracy – although considering the quantity of news published, most titles are surprisingly accurate.

In the digital age, there is a demand for eyeballs. Web traffic and other online metrics have become the way in which success is measured. But this popularity contest is not all good.

Dan Matthews has worked as an editor and writer across numerous publications and edits his own, entrepreneur-focused site, MinuteHack. Dan says that the amount of content has increased while the numbers of people employed to create and curate it has fallen.

"Digital has vastly increased the amount of content being produced, created tough competition in the form of blogs – that have grown into the likes of The Huffington Post and Buzzfeed – but it's also crashed the value of editorial," he explains.

The more traffic a site receives, the more times its adverts will be displayed. But in such an environment, editorial is largely seen as a cost. Dan says that media owners often look for ways to create content very cheaply or for free.

"Teams are tiny now as editorial budgets are slashed," he says. "Media owners have to think of innovative ways to generate more content, so rely on contributions, sponsored copy and stripped-down pieces like listicles," he says.

For James Hurley of The Times, digital has been a mixed blessing. "On one hand, it's great, as you can have a more direct relationship with readers through social media and engage with them in the comments section. But it has also eroded real journalism in a lot of places, with the rise of clickbait, fake news and more and more journalists who are chained to their desks," he says.

So, if the state of modern media is less than appetising, why are people still so attracted to it?

"To be honest, I think I became a journalist because I didn't want to have to only do one thing every day," says Madeleine Cuff, deputy editor of BusinessGreen. "I'm a geek, I've always loved reading and learning and, to me, journalism always seemed the one career where you would have a great excuse to try out new things and meet interesting people."

Madeleine says she entered the profession with her eyes wide open and that the downsides of the job are well known.

"In terms of how it has turned out, all the people who warned me of the pitfalls of journalism as a career have turned out right. Yes, it's an unstable industry, the pay isn't as much as in other sectors and competition is high for every job," she adds.

Journalism is, in many ways, fuelled by the passion and energy of those who perform it. Journalists are curious people who want to explore and even, perhaps, change the world, and this career gives them the chance to do those things.

"Despite the ups and downs, I'm still having fun, meeting inspiring people and working with some of the smartest minds around. I'm also incredibly lucky to have nabbed a job in a sector I genuinely think is the most important debate in the world right now, so I get the bonus of feeling like I'm doing something important, every day," concludes Cuff.

Press releases and news quotas

Something that journalists entering the profession soon discover is just how much the PR industry impacts upon the news agenda through the issuing of press releases.

A lot of news stories published by the media, including in national titles, are written entirely off the back of a press release without any major changes or, indeed, fact checking. I've personally worked in many editorial teams where this was common practice, as have most journalists. It's generally not particularly enjoyable work – turning press releases into news is rather dull. When you're working in such a team, you are typically judged by the number of stories you publish. The editorial team has a quota to fulfil and usually their email inboxes are the first place they look and their main resource.

The reason for this has been highlighted above; publications constantly need lots of content and press releases offer a cheap way of producing it. For business owners who want to see their stories included into these quotas, the best advice has been given in previous chapters – learn to write the news and ensure the journalist can complete the package. Some journalists do request extra information after a release has been sent and, if this is the case, reply quickly, or your name won't be on their list of sources for long.

Journalists vs PRs

Perhaps understandably, the relationship between PRs and journalists can sometimes be rather strained.

But blame for the decline of the media cannot be placed at the feet of the PR industry. Many of my colleagues have rather more sympathy for PR people than we might sometimes like to admit. There are good PRs doing a sterling job for their clients. But the industry is very mixed and entrepreneurs should be wary of engaging the wrong PR company.

As James Hurley at The Times points out, many journalists are of the view that some PR agencies are very good at winning business but not so good at representing their clients. "Of course, there are some very good PR people who would be horrified by this, but there are too many agencies willing to charge clients thousands of pounds a month and then put people who are in their first job on the account. They are told to 'hit the phones', without being properly briefed," James says.

Journalists often ignore their phones and Madeleine Cuff offers reasons why. "Recently, I've had a spate of PRs calling me about an email release they sent 10 mins beforehand. I can't tell you how annoying this is. I don't need a phone call to repeat what's already in an email to me - particularly if I haven't even had time to read it yet. It makes you feel constantly hounded, and is a real professional turn-off," she says.

It's also quite common to be offered interviews with entrepreneurs that you've already spoken to. This happens to me quite often and I am by no means the only one.

"The most annoying thing is when they don't do their homework. It takes five seconds to Google your client and realise that I've written about the company before and that was only a month ago," says Rebecca Burn-Callander.

But, striking a more diplomatic note, Burn-Callander adds: "It's symbiotic, and good PRs and good journalists understand that we need to work together to find the best stories. That said, both sides can annoy the crap out of each other when things don't go their way, but the important thing is to communicate and explain why certain decisions have been made."

I would never tell an entrepreneur not to hire a PR agency. But I would recommend they ask a few journalists for their opinion before doing so. Most of all, I'd recommend they understand their role in generating media coverage for their business. Pretty much all journalists agree that the role of the PR person isn't the most important thing. The most important thing is the subject, and that's you.

"It's frustrating, but sometimes you get midway through a news story and realise it doesn't stand up to scrutiny, or you'll do an interview where the subject is dull or reticent on details and it's not worth writing up," says Cuff.

CHAPTER 8 EXERCISES

#1 Find a journalist and offer buy them a drink or meal so you can ask them about their work. Try to understand what motivates them and how you might be able to help them.

#2 Make a list of journalists on Twitter or another social media platform and follow a few closely to see what they like to write about.

#3 Consider offering a journalist some freelance work as your company blogger, media trainer or advisor.

CHAPTER 9

IT'S TIME TO MAKE YOUR COMPANY FAMOUS

If you've read the previous nine chapters properly and completed all of the exercises, you'll now have a clear idea of how to gain press and publicity for your business. However, call me a sceptic, but I rather suspect that you've not completed all the exercises at this point. I've therefore added them all below.

The number one reason...

Throughout this book, I've given you lots of things to do and suggested reasons why some people become more famous than others. There are many things all media players need to get right – a good personal story, areas of expertise and high quality pictures being a few examples.

But I've left out what is surely the most important factor until the end: effort.

The reason some entrepreneurs become more famous than others is because they make themselves available, time and time again. I remember Martha Lane Fox, founder of Lastminute.com, saying how she "would've gone to the opening of an envelope" in the early days of her business career, so determined was she to attract attention to her company.

Being interviewed, attending photoshoots or getting up early to go to a studio for a morning slot and then heading out to events in the evening is hard work.

Right at the start of this book, I warned you that PR is not something you can outsource completely. You can certainly bring in some help - a good writer is one option or, indeed, a PR professional. You might even consider working with one of the many unemployed former journalists out there. But you will have to take the lion's share of the workload and, ultimately, be responsible.

Entrepreneurs must also display courage. If TV news wants to speak to you tonight, will you do it? The answer needs to be 'yes'. You need to jump in with both feet and worry what they'll ask you later. Nobody is ever completely ready. We are all a work in progress. The best way to become a media performer is to perform in media. Make yourself available. Put yourself out there and learn in the spotlight.

Using the techniques and know-how contained in this book you can make your company famous. Very best of luck. You can do it.

Jon Card

Acknowledgments

I should also say a special 'thank you' to Guy Pattison and Will Hill at Stronger Stories, which run the Clean and Cool missions. Guy and Will use the Hero's Journey story format, outlined in this book, to teach entrepreneurs how to pitch to investors and tell better stories about themselves. While I was aware of the Hero's Journey and how it can be used to describe entrepreneurial stories, listening to Guy and Will's seminars was highly valuable and helped crystallise much of my thinking. It also helped me to realise that there are many parallels between pitching for investment and communicating with the media. If you can do one of these well, you can most likely do the other successfully, too.

Some well-respected journalists agreed to offer their insights for this book. They are James Hurley, enterprise editor at The Times, Emma Sheppard, freelance writer and content co-ordinator at The Guardian, Dan Matthews, editor of MinuteHack and freelance writer for Forbes and the Daily Telegraph, Rebecca Burn-Callander, former enterprise editor at the Daily Telegraph and freelance journalist and Madeleine Cuff, deputy editor of Business Green.

The book also contains a number of chapters which have been written in collaboration with my wife and business partner Corinne Card, who has worked as a journalist across the national press. She was also the principal person for 'getting press for Andy' and knows a huge amount about PR, SEO and all things content and web. Together, we have been able to define what does and doesn't work in media land.

THE EXERCISES

Chapter one exercises

#1 Read a 'decent' newspaper every day. I actually recommend a print version because you can read paper faster than on a screen and you're also more likely to read a broader mix of stories. Consider the role of the journalist in each story's creation and ask yourself: who helped them to write this and how?

#2 Explain in plain English what your company actually does. Try telling someone unconnected to your industry what you do. Do they understand? Can you tell someone in less than ten seconds?

#3 Make a short list of all the acronyms and jargon used in your business. Define them. Try to discuss your work without using any jargon. Be aware of them the next time you're talking to an outsider.

Chapter two exercises

#1 Consider the Hero's Journey. Work through each of the nine parts. Try to define your call to adventure, compelling villain, allies and onwards, moving through every stage of the journey. Don't worry if some parts are less clear than others. Return to this exercise regularly.

#2 Look for examples of the Hero's Journey in films, TV, books and, of course, in newspapers. Start noting your own examples.

#3 Attempt to write your own Hero's Journey story, similar to those above - about 500 to 700 words. If you're not a great writer, get some help, but try to use your own words as much as possible.

#4 Think about how you are helping your clients or customers. Have you become the mentor? Try another version of the Hero's Journey where your customer is the hero and you are the mentor.

Chapter three exercises

#1 Examine the headlines in the newspapers and magazines you'd like to appear in. What sort of verbs, nouns and adjectives do they use? Now create some headlines for your business.

#2 Be interviewed. Either find a journalist and beg/pay them to interview you, or ask a member of your team to ask you lots of questions and record your answers. Read over your quotes - are you happy with how you sound?

#3 Create a batch of quotes about your business, industry and main interests.

#4 Review the press releases and media dispatches you have sent out to date. Look at each of the components - headlines, quotes, pictures. Are they good enough for a journalist to use?

Chapter four exercises

#1 Take a look at any photos you've previously sent to the press. Were they professional, high resolution and illustrative?

#2 Start to plan your photoshoot. Look at the pictures in your desired newspapers and magazines for inspiration.

#3 Seek out the right photographer for you. I strongly recommend someone with experience of working with the national media.

#4 Get a photoshoot!

Chapter five exercises

#1 Work on some killer sentences about yourself, similar to those in this section. Define yourself succinctly with credibility and authority.

#2 Try out #journorequest, HARO, Response Source and JournoLink.

Chapter six exercises

#1 Is there anything extreme, unusual or exciting about your company? Biggest? Fastest? Oldest? First to market? Can these claims be proven?

#2 Try writing a news story about your business, based on what you've learned.

#3 Build a forward features calendar, including awareness dates and known industry events as well as any upcoming dates others might not have noticed, which you could prepare content around.

Chapter seven exercises

#1 Think of three ways you could encourage journalists to link to your website from their publication

#2 Consider the content on your website. How useful is it?

#3 If a journalist wanted to use you as a source, how could you help them? What are you expert in? What insider knowledge do you possess?

Chapter eight exercises

#1 Find a journalist and offer buy them a drink or meal so you can ask them about their work. Try to understand what motivates them and how you might be able to help them.

#2 Make a list of journalists on Twitter or another social media platform and follow a few closely to see what they like to write about.

#3 Consider offering a journalist some freelance work as your company blogger, media trainer or advisor.

THE CHIEF STORYTELLERS' PROGRAMME

'An audacious plan to make entrepreneurs famous'

The Chief Storytellers' Programme is for ambitious CEOs, managing directors and company founders who want to power their enterprises through press and publicity. The programme enables leaders to create an influential media presence and change the world.

It ensures that they master their own story and become the chief storyteller of their organisation. Participants will appear in the national and international media, walk onto the biggest stages and see very large doors open in front of them.

The programme is limited to 100 entrepreneurs, who will be vetted to ensure they are ready for this offer. Those selected will receive bespoke media advice, mentoring, training and hands-on support with both content creation and strategy. They'll also be joining a network of other ambitious entrepreneurs with big plans and ideas.

Those who secure a place on this programme will become the chief storyteller of their business.

What the programme includes:
- Major press opportunities and a publication guarantee
- Interview training for print, radio and TV
- Professional photoshoot conducted by a seasoned Fleet Street photographer
- Hands-on media training and advice
- Key media materials and story creation
- Story development and Hero's Journey
- Networking with other famous entrepreneurs

Want to find out more?
Simply email Jon Card joncard23@gmail.com with the subject line 'CHIEF STORYTELLER' and we'll send you more information.

Printed in Great Britain
by Amazon

36061112R00085